Memoirs by Patricia L. Brooks

Gifts of Sisterhood: Journey from Grief to Gratitude

Three Husbands and a T...

Sick as My Secrets

Write the Memoir You're Afraid to Write

Write the Memoir You're Afraid to Write

Patricia L. Brooks

BROOKS GOLDMANN PUBLISHING

Scottsdale, AZ

Write the Memoir You're Afraid to Write

Copyright 2024 by Patricia L. Brooks
www.writethememoiryoureafraidtowrite.com

This book is a work of nonfiction. The events and experiences detailed herein are all true and have been faithfully rendered by the author to the best of her ability. No part of this publication may be reproduced stored in a retrieval system, or transmitted in any form or by any means, electronic, mechanical, or digital, including photocopying, recording, taping, scanning or otherwise without the express written permission of the author.

This publication is designed to provide accurate and authoritative information in regard to the subject matter covered. It is sold with the understanding that neither the author nor publisher is engaged in rendering legal or other professional services.

The author has made her best effort to prepare this book, but makes no representations or warranties with respect to the accuracy or completeness of its contents.

All rights reserved.

Manufactured in the United States of America.

For more information
Brooks Goldmann Publishing, LLC
www.brooksgoldmannpublishing.com

Book Shepherd Ann Narcisian Videan, ANVidean.com
Cover design by Kristi Wayland, electronicinkaz.com

1. Nonfiction 2. Self-help 3. How-to
Write the Memoir You're Afraid to Write / Patricia L. Brooks

ISBN: 979-8-9915962-0-6 (paperback)

Library of Congress Control Number: 2024920453

Also available in e-book.

First Brooks Goldmann Publishing Company, LLC
trade paperback edition September 2024.

I dedicate this book to all those who support me as a facilitator
of memoir writing workshops, online and in-person,
for libraries, writing groups, community venues,
and the Piper Center for Creative Writing
at Arizona State University.

Table of Contents

Dedication		
Storytelling Introduction		1
Bring Your Past to Life	Chapter 1	11
It's Your Story	Chapter 2	21
Preserve Your Stories	Chapter 3	29
Bare Your Soul	Chapter 4	37
Transformation	Chapter 5	47
Themes and Threads	Chapter 6	61
Necessities	Chapter 7	71
"Waste" Time Creating	Chapter 8	77
Driving Ambition	Chapter 9	89
Journal to Write	Chapter 10	99
Creativity	Chapter 11	111
Success	Chapter 12	121
Break the Rules	Chapter 13	129
Audience	Chapter 14	139
Endless Homework	Chapter 15	153
Psychology of Storytelling	Chapter 16	165
Why a Writing Coach?	Chapter 17	177
Writing Nonfiction	Chapter 18	185
The Author Interview	Chapter 19	191
Networking for Authors	Chapter 20	201
Age, a Gift to My Writing	Chapter 21	213

Appendices:

Author Platform	Appendix 1	225
Book Proposal Sample	Appendix 2	229

Acknowledgements	247
Author's Request	249
Book Club Discussion Questions	251
About the Author	

Storytelling

Truth: If you do not tell the truth about yourself, you cannot tell it about other people.

—Virginia Wolf, British writer

Stories come to us in social settings of all kinds: around the dinner table, at a family reunion, during a wedding or a funeral. They show up by happenstance while conversing with someone you knew many years ago.

Mr. Mayor

One of those stories came to me after recently learning my dad was almost elected mayor of my hometown. I didn't know he had ever run for public office.

My dad, Bob, was a political outspoken man and the union steward for his local longshoremen's union in northern Michigan. Unbeknownst to me, at one time, he became a candidate in a local election. As the story goes, he tied in the mayoral race 266 to 266 with Mr. Carlson, a local businessperson. This story intrigued. My dad was what you would call a blue-collar guy, not one who fits the stereotype of a local public servant. He did manual labor, some supervising, and a lot of hard physical work. A rugged guy, he did not mind getting his hands dirty.

The city council accomplished the final decision to break the tie with a coin toss that determined the outcome of the election. In small towns in America in the 1960s, this was not unusual or illegal. Both candidates agreed. My dad was well-known as a staunch Democrat and Mr. Carlson leaned Republican. The council asked Mr. Carlson, the current mayor, to make the call. He chose heads and flipped the coin. Heads it was. Mr. Carlson remained in office.

My dad never ran for public office again, although he spoke quite verbosely about his liberal views. If he had become mayor, things would have been quite different for us growing up as the mayor's girls, for good or bad. To my knowledge, he never discussed this again with anyone, certainly not his children. We learned about it fifty years later from a local town historian. Unfortunately for me and my sisters, he couldn't share this story with us. He died in 1986.

Telling tales is an opportunity to pass on knowledge, share history, or entertain with a personal narrative. Often, narratives are educational for the author, too, because they are self-reflective. It can be cathartic for the storyteller, and therapeutic for the listener. When you share them, you interpret your experiences for your readers. My dad losing the mayoral race meets all these criteria for a narrative account.

Storytelling is universal, passed down to you from the time you are a child until late in life. You hear tales from your parents, your grandparents, and other people who impact your life.

Since I write and publish memoirs, I keep in mind the various parts of a story:

- The framework—where the adventure begins.
- What it is like for the protagonist.
- What sets the tone for the story?
- The confrontation or the event.
- What turns the author's world upside down, for the good or the bad?
- Finally, the resolution—how it all works out.

You can tell your stories to the best of your ability with what you know. You share how you understand and remember them, or how you heard or received them. It is natural to remember in story form since much is in your subconscious.

I recommend that writer's journal. By keeping notes, you bring it all back to the front of the brain, then to the heart, and finally to the written word on the page. You learn from telling your stories, even those you have not experienced firsthand. They impact you in many ways, such as the story of Mr. Mayor. It empowers you when you convey your ideas.

Sharing your stories is extremely effective when you:
- Choose to educate from personal experience.
- Acknowledge how it changed your life by being transformed or enlightened.
- Tell the story in vivid detail.
- Engage the listener with your passion.

They can then imagine the story from your words and through your emotions. Your audience is impacted by your truth. After learning the story about my dad's mayoral race, I felt a deeper respect for his determination to do more with his life, and thus more with mine too.

The scary truth

For ten years, I taught Principles of Marketing part-time at Arizona State University (ASU). The university required all business students take MKT 200. One of my favorite case studies in the textbook recalled one I had lived through decades earlier, the demise of the Joseph Schlitz Brewing Company.

Schlitz fired my former husband in 1976. He mistakenly told off one of the executives in the company at a marketing meeting in Milwaukee. He drank too much and, that day, shared his ideas on how to solve their dirty little secret of watering down their beer. Although he told the wrong person, he believed he knew what they needed to do to beat Budweiser, an ongoing battle they had fought for decades.

Prosecutors later proved Schlitz tampered with their famous recipe by watering down the beer to compete with Budweiser in price and for the number one spot. They sued the company and took it to court. Some Schlitz executives went to jail for their crimes. We moved on to Arizona and read about this in *The Wall Street Journal*. My husband initially received a subpoena to go back to Milwaukee to testify, but in the end, he didn't have to return for the trial.

By the time I taught at ASU, my students would benefit from my first-hand experience with this case. They asked me many questions about life with Schlitz: my husband's job, the people we met, and what it was like for him to work for a beer company in the 1970s. Some of them had never heard of the company. This case generated a good deal of high-energy debate in the classroom twenty-five years later. Most of the textbook's information supported my personal story and perspective.

Stories naturally have a beginning, a middle, and an end. You retain the past (memories), pay attention to your present (intuition), and anticipate the future (vision). You go forward and transform your perspective with the storyline. You keep them alive as your truth if you tell them repeatedly.

I shared the Schlitz scandal many times, socially and in the classroom. This tale never got old for my students. It spoke to crime and corporate greed and followed my mantra to entertain and educate.

The compelling memoir

To write a compelling memoir, it's essential to consider the following:
- Tell the truth.
- Write because you must. It is who you are and satisfies a need to say what you want to say.
- Learn to love a true story, a memoir, biography, or a nonfiction account.
- Value the compelling memoir that comes from your soul.

If possible, draft edgy stories, not those leaving out details that may offend or make it difficult to read. These important stories may help others and change lives. The goal is to educate others and make people aware of opportunities that can impact their lives. My passion and purpose as a memoirist is to help others. For you, this may differ.

A story might be of good fortune or bad, a disaster or a bizarre instance, or a circumstance in which the hero had no control. The author might quest to understand life better. Whatever the case, the writer must give readers stories they cannot stop reading until they finish. Ones the readers will love. Gripping stories of real life.

Memoirs are stories of true-life experiences. That does not mean they are easy to write. They require much of the same structure, research, and rewriting of any fiction book. Through the words of a memoir writer, you feel their trauma and devastation, grasp their exhilaration, or live their joy and sadness.

In memoirs, your audience expects you to bring them to a prominent level of understanding through your experiences. My memoirs include trauma and recovery, grief and acceptance, domestic violence and love addiction, post-traumatic stress, forgiveness, alcoholism, and spiritual transformation. My readers absorb my perspectives in those situations. I crafted a compelling memoir each time, not by holding back, but by going deep into my soul. With selective and enthusiastic words, I put them in the room, in the car, or in the scene at that specific moment in time. You can bring your story to life this way too.

Characters

As the main character in your story, you know the angle for your life. In my second memoir, I did not show up as the domestic violence survivor many imagined: a young woman with children, no job, and a financial dependency on her abuser. I lived as a successful businesswoman, financially dependent, and single with no children. The book is not a typical domestic violence story. I wrote about my decades of love addiction before the physical violence with my abuser occurred. I analyzed my self-destructive behaviors, the emotional and psychological abuse I endured for decades, and what part I played. I knew the time was right to launch my story when I felt like an outsider looking in and could be objective. What is your good fodder for a memoir?

As the protagonist, you are the main character and the foundation of the memoir. It is critical to go deep with this type of detail. Be genuine and completely honest. If you tell the truth, it makes the story more intriguing. Such depth became possible for me after a good deal of therapy and reflective writing in my journal.

I wrote my abuse story a decade after the assault took place. I could not write my memoir when it lay too fresh and raw in my soul. Your best and honest perspective will not be there for the audience if you do not exhibit patience. It only arrives when things have settled and you understand, accept, and forgive. Then you can share the situation in your writing.

Themes

While your story has themes and threads running through it, the main theme is the core of the story.

That focus allows you begin writing or for the words to flow soon after the theme becomes clear. If you are not sure, begin first by searching your soul and journaling to jump-start your thoughts. All of this may be debated in a review, or by your readers, so know your themes and write to them. Do not be swayed by the critics, be they in your head or otherwise. This is your story.

I crafted my first memoir, *Gifts of Sisterhood: Journey from Grief to Gratitude*, with the theme of grief and loss. The threads of dying and sibling relationships streamed out from the main theme. Additional themes of family and coming of age wove their way throughout the book. I shared some of my ideas with my younger sister before she died. She encouraged me to draft our story. Early on, it was obvious to me I would write—with her in mind—about love, friendship, compassion, and courage. These later became chapter headings.

I wrote my second memoir, *Three Husbands and a Thousand Boyfriends*, around the themes of trauma, recovery, and survival. The threads of love addiction, domestic violence and post-traumatic stress, relationships, and grief wield their way through the book. These pieces evolved as I wrote. They needed nurturing with more thought and rewrites.

My third memoir, *Sick as My Secrets*, focuses on the themes of alcoholism and recovery, and faith and God. The threads are sobriety, relationships, grief, growth, transformation, and spirituality. It became clear to me as I wrote that breaking my anonymity and telling my recovery story could help others as a worthy tale of spiritual quest and growth. This memoir completed my trilogy on recovery and transformation.

The goal of a memoir is often to offer enlightenment and understanding of the main theme, and to help others in some way. The reader decides, in reviews, if the author addressed their theme and threads. You know this happens when you sense a feeling of accomplishment. Eventually, you succeed if you achieve what you set out to do. You write for yourself with the reader in mind.

The overall main theme of survival hovers over all three of my memoirs. The main themes of surviving grief, an assault, and alcohol abuse parallel one another. Each journey culminates with a satisfactory ending. I demonstrate change and live a better life for my sister in book one, break the cycle of abuse and forgive with book two, and witness my writing as cathartic and helpful with book three. The stories are not only about me, but they are also about our culture and our fellow citizens.

In memoir, you look for things that happened to you, how you reacted to them, what insight you now have from those experiences, and what awakened in you. Be it anger or love, hate or passion, you look for the patterns in your life and address them.

All the decisions I made are key choices and critical to where I am today. They illustrate the challenges I overcame and comprise my common threads.

Plot lines

When writing memoir, your madness follows a plot. It lives in the structure of the book and the things you delve into, as well as the things you leave out. It exists in the heart-wrenching moments your themes relate. A memoir is not about every little detail of your childhood. Only the truly attention-getting spheres serve up a lesson learned or a relatable tidbit.

It is important to select one or two later-in-life moments to drive home a main point. For me, I recounted meeting my current husband after remaining single for twenty-five years following two failed marriages in my twenties. As I wrote in my second memoir, after many boyfriends, failed relationships, and an assault in a domestic violence relationship, my story has a successful conclusion.

Try working with an upswing and a positive take on the story by doing the following:
- Give the reader a sense of growth, change, and transformation.
- Share hope with your audience.
- Delve into what it takes to reach that point.
- Produce a strong teaser in the first chapter.

Settings and descriptions

It is just as important in a memoir as it is in a novel to describe your setting, place, and time. Describe these in detail to allow your audience to experience each moment with you.

A small detail can turn an effective story into a cliffhanger if told properly, with all the enthusiasm and passion possible. I recommend present tense. The reader experiences its immediacy and personal relevance. You are deepening the details of your writing with the correct and best detail.

To prepare, do the following:
- Close your eyes and feel the scene to remember it.
- Feel yourself in that sad or happy occasion.
- Use all your senses to transport you back and experience the emotion.
- Scribble notes in a journal entry when they arise.
- Draw pictures to help with your visualization.
- Select the best details as they jump out at you.

Dialogue

I love dialogue in memoirs, but I do not want to only read dialogue, especially when it is lengthy. You can make these conversations work by combining your memory of that time with what you now know. If you choose to leave out dialogue in your chapters, your reader will experience the daunting task of plowing through the narrative. Dialogue makes the memoir come alive just as it does in a novel. It activates the sense of perceiving with the mind's eye.

Within reason, so as not to make sweeping assumptions about the people in the dialogue, stay true to yourself and the story. Do your best to construct the dialogue. Use whatever comes to mind to make the scene come to life. You might add an author's note at the end of the book, a disclaimer on your desire to be as authentic as possible with the dialogue. Bring to your memoir the situations and the scenes you recollect.

To hear your own voice, ask these questions in your journal:

How was I shaped by the circumstances of my life?
- Go even deeper into your topics.
- Journal honestly each morning.
- Accept who you were and who you are now.

What did I decide to do about those situations?
- Acknowledge your difficulties which form the arc of the story.
- Deliberately, but gently, lay the foundation for the rest of the story.

What did I learn from the crest of the story, the turning point?
- How to live a better life?
- How to pray?
- How to talk to God?
- How to be grateful?
- How to change?

What did I learn, what did I do, what happened next?
- The best questions for the memoir writer.

- These are straightforward and generate writing prompts.

What do I do or seek to learn today?
- Write on this question for days.
- Seek opportunities to serve your community.
- Read articles and books on your topics and become teachable.

What changed me and what am I going to do to change things going forward?
- Ask this question as a new writer.
- Address it as a person with a fresh attitude and outlook on life.
- Do not be afraid to speak out.

The End

Approach your memoir as a work of art and a feat of creativity as any novelist, artist, or playwright would do. Writing is hard, wonderful, and fun. It deserves respect no matter what genre. Writing from memory is creative and a learned skill. It needs time to rise and be kneaded before you put it aside so it can rise into its magic. Wait for the right time to send it to the editor. That may be a few weeks or a few months. The time to birth the baby is different for all of us. For me, it is after many rounds of edits, proofreads, and critiques by me, my critique group, and an editor and her helpers.

1. Bring Your Past to Life

The past should be a springboard, not a hammock.

— Edmund Burke, Irish statesman

To bring your past to life, you need to consider poignant questions so your subconscious can work for you. By taking stock of where you have been and where you are now, you develop the stories that need to be told. Ponder the following questions as you choose stories for your memoir. My reflections support you to journal first for clarification and write later. The ten lessons enhance the examples.

What comes back to you repeatedly?

Memories of my hometown, St. Ignace, fifty miles south of the Canadian border, come back to me often. Located in the Upper Peninsula of Michigan, it is green, wooded, and pristine with clear water and sandy beaches. This area sits at the eastern end of the Upper Peninsula, the part of Michigan most think belongs to Canada. The Mackinac Bridge—a mammoth two-tower, five-mile expansion bridge—hovers over the point where Lake Michigan and Lake Huron meet at the Straits of Mackinac. This bridge welcomes you to the North Country, a picturesque place seen in most travel shots of Michigan.

Various scenes of lakes, beaches, watercraft, wooded trails, and a quieter life reoccur often in my mind's eye. You won't see any stoplights in the town. Wi-Fi keeps it current. Some of the same restaurants survive. Franchises creep in to change the landscape. St. Ignace represents quaint small-town Americana.

Even though I left for college in 1968 and never lived there again, it will always be home. I return often to see friends and family and soak in my fix of its beauty. Some things have changed; some have not. I find it a special and beautiful place.

Lesson #1: Bring the reader's emotions out and engage them in dramatic scenes.

What stories disturb you in the middle of the night?

I need to tell the stories that illuminate how much my life has changed in adulthood since leaving Michigan and how much growth has transpired within me. Therefore, I yearn to go back and visit.

Happy memories such as sledding, skating, beachcombing, and living near the Great Lakes come to mind. Some of my happy times include an outing with the Camp Fire Girls hunting mushrooms in the woods, and birthday parties during wintry days with my friends. I cherish these memories now after being in the Southwest desert for more than forty years. They tie me to the water and the seasons that enfold the town.

Life there wasn't perfect. We experienced long, rough winters and tough times. As with other parts of the Midwest, many families faced high unemployment and personal struggles. In the end, I choose to remember those early days with nostalgia.

Some of my most vivid memories include:
- A new Norman Rockwell calendar is hung each January.
- A red rotary-dial telephone on the kitchen wall.
- Breakfast of lake perch and eggs on the stone grill in the backyard.
- White ice skates with baby-blue laces gliding across the school rink.

- Running down the hill to Lake Huron for a swim.
- My green birthday decorations and cake on St. Patty's Day.

Lesson #2: Build trust with your readers by describing and showing them who you really are.

What memories are important to you and need to be shared?

My memories of friendship, and competition between the kids in the neighborhood, come to mind—a bond we shared from the First Ward. The joy and isolation of living at Graham's Pointe, that small part of town that juts out into Lake Huron at the end of State Street, was dear to me. Our beach area sported a few houses in the fifties and sixties, except for the summer cabins that closed Labor Day weekend. Life was good.

I flashback to:
- Our Collie-Airedale dog, Fuzzy, taking rocks from Lake Huron to the shoreline.
- Swimming Memorial Day weekend in jeans and a sweatshirt when the weather still remained cold.
- Working the night shift as a summer waitress at a truck shop to earn school money.
- Watching the aurora borealis to the north on a summer night while sitting close to my boyfriend.
- Listening to Detroit Tigers baseball games with my boyfriend in his truck at Sand Bay.
- Bonfires at night on the beach while with my friends at the sand dunes on Lake Michigan west of town.

Lesson #3: Lead with a laugh or humorous story as soon as you can.

What is your purpose in telling these stories?

My purpose, in all my memoirs, has been to preserve the innocence of those times while sharing my truth to help others. With a sense of camaraderie and joy in 2018, I headed home to my fiftieth class reunion. While there, I launched my third memoir, *Sick as My Secrets*, at several events. Its tales reflect a simpler time when skating faster than the night before gave you bragging rights. Or when navigating freshly fallen snow required snowshoes.

I have always been proud of where I came from, never denying growing up in the woods of a town with fewer than three thousand people.

This information is critical to who I am and, therefore, to my reader. The place did not have dial telephones until 1971 when Gerald Ford, a Michigander, became president and removed us from obscurity with one decision. Our town was the last place in Michigan to use the old Private Branch Exchange (PBX) system that mechanically switched to connect calls. President Ford wanted all of Michigan to be in the 20th century.

Some of my memories still remain fifty-plus years later:
- An old-time Fourth of July parade.
- The glistening stained glass of the Methodist church window.
- The breathtaking view of Mackinac Island across Moran Bay.
- The McCann Street school skating rink.
- Big waves at the sand dunes of Lake Michigan a few miles from my hometown.
- Chief's Drive-In for a burger with my boyfriend.
- Silver and turquoise jewelry at the Indian village.
- Smelt fishing in Foley's Creek in early spring.

Lesson #4: Think like a fiction writer with descriptive scenes, an arc, and a hook.

Who provides background for you?

You can look to both friends and family to provide primary firsthand research. I am fortunate to be in touch on Facebook with about a dozen women from my high school class of 1968. They still live in my hometown or nearby in Michigan and support my writing with their memories. We shared cheerleading, senior band concerts, and parade marches. We served as class officers, planned junior prom together, and stood up in each other's weddings after high school. As adults, we have shared so much more. Especially grief.

Family may be unavailable to help. Fortunately, they aren't essential. My parents are gone now, along with my younger sister. My older half-sister left home when I was twelve years old. Absent during my teenage years, she can truly contribute little, if anything. I've asked very few questions of my other sister or my Michigan-based cousins. We've lived in different states since we were teenagers.

I offer you these reminders:
- Your truth is what matters.
- Do not apologize for your stories.
- Trust your intuition.
- Follow your intentions.
- Do not fear retaliation.
- Be bold and brave.

Lesson #5: Stay relevant with your growth and understanding today.

What do you really want to say?

While I share my stories about the Mackinac area, my hometown, my youth, and my teenage years, my memoirs also reflect my purpose. Through the lens of my later years, with my experience, growth, and transformation, I wrote to say what I wanted to say and what needed to be said.

I suggest the following to help you do the same:
- Brainstorm with yourself. Write lists of keywords. Develop phrases.
- Be determined to tell your stories in your own words with your voice.
- Be open and consider all feedback before making choices.
- Be willing to share hard-learned lessons and the solutions drawn since.
- Write the way you speak.
- Close your eyes to trigger all your senses.
- Later, read what you wrote aloud.
- Read other memoirs for ideas.
- Add your own wit.
- Punctuate your stories with surprise and suspense.

Lesson #6: Keep relevant to your purpose and spice it up where you can.

Are you willing to explore your feelings deeply?

I learned from publishing three memoirs that intense soul-searching drives to the heart of the story. To do this, I pray about my writing, then begin the process of listening to my inner voice. The result? Pure and authentic stories straight from the heart.

At times, my process requires going deep within to gather what is necessary to finish my thoughts. I went there without hesitation. It takes concentration and quiet meditation to do this. Even if it means uncovering an unpopular truth, I go there. I explore my feelings and allow myself a greater understanding of my life.

As part of your process, I recommend you undertake the following critical tasks:

- Thoroughly understand the main theme of your book.
- Identify the threads that weave your theme through your story.
- Listen to your heart and soul in mindful moments.
- Follow your intuition, that strong feeling in your gut.
- Do not be afraid of what you hear or see.
- Document immediately when you know something is written for your story.

Lesson #7: Write for the reader as well as for yourself.

What events happened in your childhood to change your life?

Many things happened, but a major change came when my half-sister, six years older than me, married and moved out when I was twelve. This incident changed our family dynamics. As the oldest one at home, I automatically took on a different role. I inherited my own bedroom instead of sharing one with three sisters. My parents built a new bedroom at the front of the house that spring. My two younger sisters took it over, and the situation created heaven for all of us. Often, I assumed the responsibility for my youngest sister and rose to the occasion. This special effort means a lot to me as she is the one who died early, at age forty-four.

My parents would say things to me like:
"You are more grown up than your friends."
"You are a leader in school."
"Your friends look up to you."
"You look older than you are."
"You are strong."
"You are a smart girl."

Lesson #8: Be honest and promise the reader your truth from your perspective.

What stories will you share to help others?

The fun and friendship I realized as a teenager added to my self-confidence in a big way and became important for me to share. I've retained many of those friendships. The sibling rivalry I experienced at home added energy to my meager existence and still surfaces occasionally.

Our family shared a worry each spring. It hovered over our household. When would the Great Lakes thaw, requiring my dad to go back to work as a tugboat captain? We depended on the union's call for all the income of the family. We gleaned wisdom from that often-stressful situation by appreciating his sacrifice. This monetary situation complicated the anxiety of my youth.

I wanted to leave as soon as I graduated from high school in 1968. I feared the dreaded "cabin fever" in winter with its sensation of walls moving in on you, suffocating even when you had fresh clean air. I experienced this form of anxiety early in life. Learning to survive the long winter challenged me.

Try these suggestions to relate to this type of frustration:
- Have empathy for your readers by drafting your stories with tact.
- Be the hero/heroine.
- Endear them to you by building trust that your facts are correct.
- Be authentic. Make your words your own.
- Never stop, slow down, block, or derail your stories or your message.
- Respect your reader's intelligence.

Your memoir stories reflect how you bring the past back to life and how your stories change you or hold you in check. Memories comprise much of what is important to you later in life. Reading other people's memories sheds light on how they preserve a life changed, yet valued, for what it offers. The reader may change in some small way because of reading your words.

Activity: Scavenger Hunt Writing Prompt

1. Visualize creating a collage for the purpose of your writing.
2. Scavenge your home, office, or community for collage ideas.
3. Paste them onto your collage poster board or use nonstick tape for your wall.
4. Copy down or photograph words, phrases, and sentences you find interesting.
5. Use conversations to collect words.
6. Build from your scraps a central theme for your writing.

2. It's Your Story

Drafting a book is an adventure. To begin with, it is a toy and amusement. Then it becomes a mistress, then it becomes a master, then it becomes a tyrant.

—Winston Churchill, British statesman, former Prime Minister of the United Kingdom.

You are subject to ethical considerations when you write, even when they are your own stories. You judge what is appropriate for you and your fellow writers by dealing with issues that arise via a clear conscience and an even clearer state of mind. It is your obligation to be true to yourself and to be authentic, while not plagiarizing others.

How do you capture your story?

Your voice is there. It's ready to use if you allow it to flow freely. This is especially true if you do not hinder your thoughts by trying to make them sound like someone else's comments.

You will do well if you:
- Write naturally.
- Find your own voice by sitting in quiet and listening to your thoughts.
- Honor your style and unique quality by analyzing your work.

- Read the works of many memoirists to see what is out there.
- Learn how others have found their voice and glean ideas from them.

Listen to your voice after you have written and revised your chapters by reading them aloud. Honor your style and be comfortable with it. As you polish your work, look for your patterns. Do not try to change anything about your voice. It is who you are, what will endear you to your readers. Fiercely maintain your high standard of writing so as not to stop your natural flow and to achieve your style.

My favorite activity is to highlight things that jump out at me when I read another's memoir. Not to copy or lift from their pages, but to remember them vividly and find them quickly when I review. I use other memoirs as a reference point and would be flattered if someone did the same with my work.

Reading the memoirs of Mary Karr and Joyce Maynard has been invaluable, as have the works of Katherine Harris, Kelly Corrigan, and Jeannette Walls. They all have such an incredible way of telling stories in their own voice yet are similar in their pursuit of truth. I love their styles and, while not copying them, I emulate their pursuit of truth.

How do you learn the craft of writing?

With many ways to learn the craft, not all opportunities out there are available to every writer or necessarily of interest to any of them.

Some suggestions:
- Take writing classes at your community college, library, or bookstore.
- Attend national writing conferences, online or in person.
- Be open and willing to learn new ways of writing dialogue or setting scenes.
- Study the concepts of memoirs and take them seriously.

- Read books on writing memoir and creative nonfiction.
- Interview others who have written memoir via phone or Zoom, or over coffee.

Even though I have a master's degree and teach at Arizona State University as an adjunct faculty member, I humbled myself and signed up for a community college writing course. This was more than twenty years ago now, when I started writing my first memoir. I had done a ton of business writing for almost twenty years. I still developed my skills and techniques and practiced my craft by embarking on unfamiliar territory.

I enjoyed the writing classes at Phoenix College for a couple of years. I pursued various workshops locally and at conferences in the western part of the country. I found writing groups in the Phoenix area and immediately contacted the Scottsdale Civic Center library regarding their offerings for aspiring authors. I searched online for speakers who facilitated writing events, not just on memoir, but nonfiction too. I investigated many of them and learned a great deal.

A few more suggestions:
- Listen intently to class conversations while attending a writing workshop.
- Participate in class with questions or stories.
- Take copious notes and learn the lessons offered.
- Do not quote the speaker verbatim.

I attended local and national conferences on many occasions, including the Desert Nights Rising Stars conference at Arizona State University, the San Diego State University Writers Conference, the Las Vegas Writers Conference, and the Willamette Writers Conference in Portland, Oregon. By attending as many sessions as possible, I soon felt like a part of the writing world. The enrichment I received went beyond advancing my skills and learning the craft of writing. I experienced the insight of fellow authors and the wisdom of the speakers. In each case, I attempted to get to know them personally through social media and conversation.

How do you know if memoir is for you?

There are three kinds of memoirs. If you study them and one calls to you, memoir is for you.
1. Complex memoir involves extensive research and historical information.
2. Single-focus memoir is in depth and at a more personal level.
3. Life story is more of a gift for a family member than a commercial work.

Consider these three options. If one rings true, you will have your answer. Take your time with this decision before you commit.

Complex memoir

This option involves extensive research to enhance your memories. My third memoir, *Sick as My Secrets*, shines here more than my first two books. It cuts across decades of time. As my spiritual transformation and recovery story, it's filled with tales that required more detail about people and places than I could readily remember.

I made phone calls, wrote letters and emails, and did online research to bring many things about the 1970s era back to life. Food, beverages, fashion, and slang comprised a big part of that research, as were places I had lived and not visited since that time. I needed to paint vivid pictures of the scenes in my stories to make them real. I also wanted to pay respect to places I had called home, the people I knew, and the spirit of that era.

Single-focus memoir

This involves taking one aspect of your life to put the spotlight on it. My second memoir, *Three Husbands and a Thousand Boyfriends*, follows this form more than the others, but they all tend to lean this way. That is what memoir is all about in the true sense of the definition. It's a focus on a single aspect of your life, an experience, or an accomplishment.

In the second memoir, I tell my story about love addiction and domestic violence. It covers more than four decades of my life and the husbands and boyfriends who crossed my path during that time. I share side comments on my career, family, alcoholism, and spirituality, but mostly stay on topic so its purpose is not lost and I can tell my story to help others.

Life story

My first memoir, *Gifts of Sisterhood: Journey from Grief to Gratitude*, exemplifies this third option, as a gift. I wrote about my relationship with my youngest sister and her courage facing lung cancer. My original goals were to leave her legacy for her sons and to discuss grief, our relationship, and the value of sibling sisterhood.

I authored the book for her two boys, who were barely teenagers at the time of her death. After publication, the book quickly became much bigger than her legacy. I began facilitating a grief workshop with our story with the book at its foundation.

Smoking was the cause of my sister's death. I worked on the Arizona Smoking Ban included on the November ballot at that time. I started my own Stop Smoking Sister campaign to honor her for quitting smoking twelve years prior to her diagnosis. When asked to do so, I continue to spread awareness on the issues of women and lung cancer and speak to groups on all aspects of a smoking addiction.

How do you authentically tell your truth?

This is the proverbial question for the memoir writer. The answer: understand your angle on life. You can tell your truth by maintaining journal entries that go deep into your soul, your story, and your topic, and by asking yourself repeatedly, "What is my angle on life?"

Consider these suggestions:
- Show your true character in your words.
- Be authentic.
- Provide as much detail as possible.

- Be fluid in your writing.
- Give your reader whatever rises to the surface.
- See in your mind's eye what lies in wait in your subconscious.

We all have a unique X-factor. Magnetism, self-confidence, social ability, charm, inner peace, intellect, or a sense of humor—it is a distinct part of our truth. Keep searching for yours and nurture it in your journal entries so it becomes valuable to your stories. Be proud of whatever yours might be.

I nurture my sense of humor and inner peace daily with my meditation, only to find that my self-confidence comes along too. In my third memoir, I shared the beginnings of my spiritual awakening and transformation. My angle on life relates to what I have learned from my mistakes. I am willing to share those lessons to help others.

What is your angle? How will you find it to bring your stories to life? If you don't have both the beginning and the end and movement in the middle, you don't have your viewpoint, your perspective. Your angle brings your premise, your outlook, into play. Strive for an element of surprise too.

Remember, a premise to your story exists. It sets your direction. You just need to find the concept. When I worked on a marketing project, we called it a *tagline* or *handle*. In the movies, it is the *concept*. I love trying to figure out the slant of the story when I see a good movie.

For those of us writing memoirs, our written words reveal our position, our dominant idea. Do not write aimlessly.

Choose from these suggestions:
- Be clear and concise.
- Be on a mission.
- Include an element of surprise.
- Create natural tension by ramping up the situation.
- Show us how you changed under pressure, stood up, and fought back.
- Make comparisons for emphasis.

To evoke imagery and emotion, consider using these comparison techniques: metaphor (curtain of night), simile (brave like a lion) and personification (the car complained). You'll notice these comparisons in the movies.

Comparison encourages attention by likening people to animals. For example, my friend, Ellen, helped me repeatedly and was as loyal as an old dog during the time of my assault, but my other "friend," Judy, continued to poke fun at the situation as selfishly as a cat. Even humor can be used to compare and lighten the load of the story. Use yourself as the brunt of the joke, rewarding the reader for listening to the horrific story in the first place.

Playing devil's advocate is another angle for your story. My recovery story, *Sick as My Secrets*, illustrates conflict and change. I refer to my therapist and my recovery sponsor whose words often opposed what I did or wanted to do.

Some tales may be quirky in nature or forbidden. Give the reader the latter for tension. My conflicts with my therapist or my sponsor did not need to be heated. They looked out for my best interests. The angle showed the opposition, serious or not, to entertain and educate the reader on recovery toward a hopeful ending.

Observing others can highlight an angle by presenting categories you don't have personal experience with. In *Gifts of Sisterhood*, I wrote about my sister's lung cancer. I shared my views with incredible openness on the way she was initially treated by the local doctors who misdiagnosed her. They did not take her seriously as a woman with health complaints. I observed the ease with which they blamed her lower back pain on her weight and stress.

I found it difficult to accept the situation when she sought help at the Mayo Clinic in Minnesota, only to learn the news she'd feared. I became obsessed with where we could take her for treatment, even investigating options in Mexico.

I could have changed the tone of my voice and my attitude about the topic of lung cancer by emphasizing the ten percent survival rate for women over forty. I did not choose that angle, but instead stayed the course. I became an advocate to create awareness of this cancer that kills twice as many women each year as breast cancer.

In the end, I wrote to my own satisfaction. I opted to take a lighthearted, humorous approach to an otherwise bleak subject. I highlighted the sense of humor we shared. She was witty and funny. I captured some of that even in those dire moments, no matter what the stories entailed.

By letting others read my work before the final editing, I was able to craft a warm and loving tribute to her for her sons. It became a book with a heart and soul of its own. This memoir took on a quest to help others and be of service to those left behind with grief.

Activity: Associations

1. Choose a noun you like—your name, for example.
2. Write it vertically down a page.
3. Begin a phrase using the first letter of each word.
4. Tell a story from your words.
5. No need to fear lack of structure.
6. Have fun and share your story.

3. Preserve Your Stories

Preservation of one's own culture does not require contempt or disrespect for others' cultures.
—Cesar Chavez, American civil rights activist

Preservation provides the key to an incredible memoir of your complex dramas, good times, and tough times. Sustain your stories. These embody the core of your memoir and the basis for your words to come alive with all their richness. By continuing to polish your stories, you will bring them to life, convey your desires, and illustrate setbacks and triumphs. Whether written decades ago or told to you by someone recently, you can add to them without embellishment yet still give them flare.

What "coming-of-age" story do you possess?

Can you tell a story about your mother or your father at your same age—distinctly different from yours but that provokes similar emotions?

Try these ideas:
- See yourself in their places by putting together a scrapbook.
- Relate to their lives in several ways through an integral thread woven in family history.

- Treasure your cultural legacy with items like dishes and by collecting recipes.
- Go digital with photos or video to help you tell the stories.

How does their coming-of-age story compare to yours? Do you have a generational story of growing up on a farm or in an inner city that can evolve into a good lead story? Some of these are easy to document; some will take a lot more time.

Find a "special shelf" for artifacts that will enhance your memory.

Consider handwriting your records to begin. Write whatever comes to you immediately to strengthen your sense of belonging.

Celebrate family traditions such as placing a flag on the front door on certain holidays or planting flowers in an old rock garden to simulate an experience of springtime.

Ask yourself these questions:
- Is my parents' story vastly different from mine?
- Can I *be* on that farm when I only know city life?
- Are interviews or photos available?
- Is my life relatable to their two-parent home versus a one-parent home?
- Do I have objects from their lives I can place near me when I write?
- Has anyone made a quilt of my cultural heritage that could be useful?

Think back to stories when you felt sibling rivalry or camaraderie, and how those similarities might integrate the threads of your memoir.

Journal about the following:
- Did you fight with your siblings?
- Were you in constant competition with them?
- Did you feel a closeness to your siblings, a bond that cannot be broken?
- Are you inspired by your siblings or motivated by their lives enough to write this all down?

Write the Memoir You're Afraid to Write

Reflect upon a lost sibling or friend and write about them. Tell us what you learned from them, especially if you were the oldest, as I did in *Gifts of Sisterhood*. My younger sister's story is as much about my appreciation of her life as it is about our relationship and the necessity to honor her. I told the story of our relationship. I told her story of courage and strength. It imparted her willingness to do anything to live a little longer for her teenagers and gave me the chance to reveal the falsehoods surrounding lung cancer.

At the time of her illness, little was being done to change the low survival rate for women. We do not talk often enough about lungs. We talk about breasts. Through this life account, I talk about lungs, her gift to us. My sister fought hard to win the odds and be one of the ten percent of women who survive. I felt compelled to tell her story. The quilts she made for all of us were always finished beautifully, and her story needed to be too. She left a legacy with her cancer battle. I deemed it essential to put it down in words to help us gain a greater understanding of these challenges.

I revised the memoir in 2021, adding additional pages on grief at the beginning of the book, and re-editing and publishing it with a new cover. This was important because memoirs are timely.

If you have cousins who lived with you or spent a lot of time with you, or a favorite aunt or uncle who helped raise you and were a part of your story, work to incorporate them into your theme. Captured truthfully, all that knowledge can provide vital information of your family history. Warm scenes at the Thanksgiving table, and a delicious meal prepared from family recipes may conjure up lasting memories for you.

For me, it is Aunt Madge's family reunions. My dad's sister, Madge, held festivities in a lovely, large, three-story home with a sprawling front porch. She offered us a wonderful Thanksgiving dinner for at least thirty family members of all ages. We played games and engaged in conversation after pie was served. No televised football games allowed.

Feel free to use these visualizations which I used for my book:
- Did you see these cousins more as sisters or brothers?
- Did you spend many holidays or summers together?
- Do you have good memories of all this family time?
- Do you long for closure within your family unit?
- Do you have relatives you feel you need to thank or apologize to?
- Do you have a family member you need to confront or question?

Whether these stories are happy, invoke humorous or sad anecdotes, or give you something else entirely, consider writing about them to make your memoir full and complete. If they impacted you in some way and you can tie them back directly to where you are today, they are invaluable. Authoring your stories inspires greater love and compassion for your flaws and mistakes.

Are you ready to proceed to other stories?

You always have more to tell and more to share. For example:
- The hard-to-tell stories that equip us with communication and thinking skills.
- The challenges you face in life become more visible.
- The painful moments that may or may not have been resolved but are clearer.
- The success stories now preserved in your mind.
- The obstacles you overcame to find peace.
- The failures that gave you the greatest life lessons.

For me, the hard-to-tell stories live in my third memoir, *Sick as My Secrets*, published in 2018. It took courage to vividly tell the story of my recovery from alcoholism and spiritual transformation that began in 1983. That memoir encompasses my ten-year drinking career yet encapsulates a lifetime of emotional and psychological torment culminating with recovery, the lessons learned, and the growth earned. I knew not to blame anyone and be responsible for my part in all the experiences and tales told. Now that I have survived more than forty years in recovery, my success story may inspire hope.

I address my life challenges—love addiction and domestic violence—in *Three Husbands and a Thousand Boyfriends*. I take the reader on my journey as I progress through that painful time in my life. I share what encouraged me to seek help and how I turned that painful time into an opportunity to help others by showing the obstacles to overcome.

A success story winds through each of my memoirs. I went into detail about my alcohol recovery, explaining the obstacles I overcame to enter a program of recovery and make sobriety and hope possible. All my memoirs take this approach, and I recommend the same to you. Failures are great teachers.

How will you face your fears with your writing?

Breaking through the silence to find clues to your past may take meditating or talking to a counselor. It requires the courage to communicate with family and friends or search your soul for your truth, to do your memoir correctly. You may not realize when you are silent that a voice inside of you wants to say something about your life's adventures. Allow yourself time to be still and quiet. Take walks and listen to yourself. Write in a journal and wait for your inner voice to speak. This will help you have clear goals and objectives and stay focused while discovering why you are the way you are.

These prompts can move you forward:
- Figure out the "hot spots" of your story, the special places that keep the reader engaged.

- Recognize the emotional beats that bring the story along at a pace that coincides with your style and voice.
- Avoid nothing that arises from your subconscious.
- Tell your story truthfully and naturally.
- Tell your story the way you experienced it and the way you remember it.
- Remember, it is your truth and your voice we want to hear when we read.
- Trust that you told your story truthfully when you said, "This is my story."

Give yourself permission to draft your story the way you know it. Never feel you are less than writers who have come before you or those taking this journey with you. Everyone starts out as a beginner in taking up the challenge to pursue their story. If you have an inkling to do so, draft your stories. If you have any desire to do so, you must write. You cannot quit. Just keep making the effort to remember as many details as possible. The more family history you know, the more you will understand yourself.

Remember not to be discouraged by a family member or friend who questions your recording of an event. It is an art and a gift to be a storyteller. If you know you are one, run with your writing. Generations to come will read your stories. For posterity, weave a great tale with each sentence.

Give lasting remarks or reflections by doing the following:
- Take immense pride in the art of storytelling and learn more about it.
- Keep your memories intact. Keep a running outline so they do not fade with time.
- Lose any fear of retaliation from anyone. Be confident in your stories.
- Be proud of what you know by summing up your key thoughts.

How will you tell your truth?

First, you will not apologize for anything you write because the truth you tell is not hurtful or vengeful of others. You were there. You saw and participated in the story and recollected it to the best of your ability. You are safe in your truth as you unleash your creativity without defaming anyone.

Next, you will learn more about yourself as you reflect and embrace a new perspective about what happened in each instance, photo, and interview. If you are true to yourself and take your writing as a serious art and service to others, your truth will not reveal itself negatively. Find out who, what, when, where, why, and how. Be an investigator.

Be descriptive in your writing and show us what happened. Capture a time and lifestyle that may be gone forever. Put us in the scene so your truth is even more believable. Do not just tell us the story—make the story come to life with vivid and active words. Read your work aloud to hear yourself describe what happened. Then close your eyes and see yourself there again. Go back to the scene if possible and describe the incidents just as you remember them. Interview others who were there. Determine how you will write from that space.

Take these suggestions as reminders. They have worked for me:

- Honor your story, your chance to inspire.
- Truth is stranger than fiction and can change lives.
- Authenticity is powerful and makes history.
- Bridge gaps with your readers. Paint your picture truthfully.

To unravel the truth of your heart, you must increasingly reveal yourself on your pages. You are peeling away the layers of the onion. Your readers will cheer for you. Be confident and don't underestimate your role as a writer. Your heart will not lead you astray if you have it in the right place. Make nothing up. Rely on your intuition as your guide. Write with fierce abandon to bring it to the world like no one else can.

The final phase of telling your truth is to commit to your "dark side" by not ignoring that "shadow self" that needs to say something too. Those parts of you take you to your depth. Do not be afraid of what you might hear, or need to hear, to solve a conflict within you. Never forget that getting deep into your story is often cathartic and healing. Remembrances are precious. Use all you can in your stories. Your writing can be powerful, inspirational, and motivational, with the ability to change lives and minds.

Readers yearn for your story and for mine. Plenty of room exists for us all to preserve and share our humanity. This genre is strengthened when we support each other to publish our memoirs instead of compete head-on. We build our connection by knowing we create a more compassionate world because of what we are writing.

Activity: What if? A process I used many times while drafting my stories.

1. Ask a fellow writer to join you in this activity.
2. Choose a hypothetical situation to explain your truth.
3. Be adventurous by testing the possibilities for a couple of days.
4. Write fiercely about what you've selected.
5. Exchange ideas about your process with your partner to stimulate discussion.
6. Enjoy rather than critique whatever information you have gleaned.

4. Bare Your Soul

I believe that man will not merely endure, he will prevail. He is immortal not because he is alone among creatures and has an inexhaustible voice, but because he has a soul.

—William Faulkner, American writer

To bare your soul is to reveal your innermost secrets and feelings to someone. Even though you might feel vulnerable, it is a freeing and rewarding experience. Memoir requires you go deep and give the reader what they want and expect. Your job: to deliver on the expectations of the reader and reveal your private thoughts and feelings. Your obligation: to confess your intimate thoughts to endear your reader.

Go beyond soul-stirring moments

- Go beyond telling what you remember or reliving a tale.
- Expand your reader's horizons by giving all you can to the story.
- Stop your readers, catch them off guard, and make them uncomfortable.
- Write whatever moves you.
- Admit you're uncomfortable even though you know you must keep writing.
- Tell your stories no matter what happens.

Incorporate all parts of your journey, including your readers' reactions. In my memoirs, I use the vulnerability angle often by owning up to feeling fear at times when writing my truth. I did this in all three of my memoirs, but especially in *Sick as My Secrets*.

Reveal the depth of your memoir

- Commit to yourself that these revelations are part of your memoir and critical to your story.
- Understand they are paramount to your success and cannot be left out.
- Reveal the difficult parts, especially to family members and friends who are involved in your account.
- Listen to your tales as they whisper in your ear or gnaw at you in the night.

In *Sick as My Secrets*, I felt uncomfortable at times, but I had to tell my recovery story. Being silent served no purpose in my mission to help others. I had a message. I risked retaliation from a few, and questions from family and friends. No matter, the truth needed to be told.

Do not hold back

Keep the faith. You have a message and a story you must get out.

- See where your purpose lies in your writing.
- Be grateful to anyone who will help you with your writing and your research.
- Lose any inhibitions getting in your way.
- Seek out those in your writing circles who want you to succeed, who'll believe in you when you're faced with obstacles and doubt.
- Give to receive.
- Associate with like-minded men and women.

Staying close to your tribe and your confidantes prepares you for upcoming reviews. Those reviews may or may not be what you expect. Everyone can learn from feedback and be selective in what to apply. It is your book, and you can have faith in your writing.

Be willing to take risks with your work

Being brave and courageous as a writer is the only way to feel confident you're using your creativity. To be anything less than a force of nature stifles you. You will surely feel disappointed if you finish a writing project any other way.

In my memoir regarding my recovery and spiritual journey, I stepped into my bravery from the first words written. I took risks to get the details of my story out. I did not cheat the reader.

Consider these suggestions to be brave:
- Read other people's work to expand your mind, regardless of genre.
- Study their style and structure to learn first and possibly emulate later.
- Consider only what feels right. This is your choice as a writer.
- Be proud of your decisions.
- Stand strong in defense of your decisions.
- Study the ways and ideas of other authors. Evaluate why they do things the way they do.
- Consider drafting book reviews for others, being gentle with criticism as you share your voice.
  - Understand what you're talking about in a review.
  - Learn how to review so you can evaluate your work too.
  - Be informed on the topic and the idea you present. Do research if you're not knowledgeable.

- Don't challenge yourself to the point of derailing yourself or your words.
- Use the philosophy of positives first and constructive criticism second.
- Read reviews, as I do, in *The New York Times*, *USA Today*, and your local newspaper.

The easiest way to review, for me and for you, is to follow what I learned many years ago in Toastmasters International. First, share the positives, the highlights of what inspired or moved you and meant a lot to you. Second, question one or two things in the book you feel are acceptable but could be improved. Last, give constructive criticism in a professional manner. I enjoy reading reviews and giving them. I try to touch on all of these aspects to make the review a quality piece, whether long or short.

Heal your past

- Determine which powerful secrets you're willing to share.
- Use them as tools, not weapons, to clarify or enhance your stories.
- Be aware of what will hurt someone and what will not by following your intuition.
- Make the best choice so you can heal and not add more anger or pain to your story.
- Use only first names and ask for permission only if you fear facing consequences.

With my memoir, *Sick as My Secrets*, I used first names to bring the reader into the scenes. I only referred to my abuser as my abuser in the chapter on my assault. I never used his name in the book. I gave him no power. When referencing my therapist, I used "my therapist," except in one instance when I used her name, Ann, as she is deceased. No harm could come.

- Always tell your story as you deem necessary for full understanding.
- Don't leave out critical details that add to the uniqueness of your story. This would cheat you and your reader.
- Be proud of writing toward your purpose.

Quiet your inner critic with your inner voice

Engage in daily affirmations before you settle into writing. These easy and healing ideas prime your mind and set you up to create. Selecting a monthly affirmation and repeating it every day has helped my writing tremendously. You help your authoritative voice by writing in your journal to clear your head about anything that's blocking you. That authoritative voice heals you and gives you strength to go on writing. Meditation reveals every issue in your soul, so you discover what you need to share. I walk and meditate to hear myself.

Writing in any genre, but especially in memoir, requires forgiveness, particularly of yourself. Nobody's perfect. You continue to make mistakes, but if you're willing to learn from them, you begin to heal and produce powerful writing. You can't forgive anyone with your words until you first forgive yourself. There's no way to shortcut this process. You'll only disappoint your readers. Being humble and admitting your mistakes endears you to them.

- Give the reader your emotional truth.
- Share your feelings.
- Bring your story to life on the page.
- Be open and honest.

The healing will come. Your readers will appreciate what you've experienced, resolved, learned, and are willing to share. They'll want more and stay engaged to finish your book.

With my last memoir, I shared all of my truth from memory. I was brutally honest about my addiction to alcohol, the consequences I faced, and what I had to do to recover from that lifestyle. The healing came when I shared my enthusiasm about my spiritual transformation. I not only resolved the story but communicated solutions to so many of my story's issues. The reader could feel uplifted from my hope.

All of us possess a dark side, a shadow self, a place we hide sometimes even from ourselves, yet a place we must go in memoir. Near the end of *Sick as My Secrets*, I focus a chapter on forgiveness. I highlight several relationships and how I chose to mend them by forgiving myself and asking for their forgiveness. This in no way disregards or condones their behavior but acknowledges my power to move forward. That chapter shows how humility can go a long way toward restoring badly broken relationships.

Go to your dark side, your shadow self

- Go to your dark side repeatedly. This is the path to authenticity.
- Don't hold back.
- Show the hope so the reader relates and receives what they want.
- Journal to find your shadow self, your primitive and negative human emotions.
- After your second draft, polish it even more. Be objective.

Everything you see in others is in yourself. You often go to great lengths to protect yourself and what you show the world. You don't want to present yourself as unflattering. You have great gifts in several areas and yet remain blind to your shadow self, your darkness.

When you go to the dark place within, you release it and see it. You become authentic in your work. You energize your creativity and awaken fresh writing possibilities. You can use your anger, envy, greed, desire, or selfishness to your advantage. You can't eliminate this shadow self, but you can see it for what it is and be a better writer.

Whatever qualities you deny in yourself you will see reflected in others. Exploring all your sides takes you deeper, igniting a profound level of writing. This action affords the chance to grow at any time and any age.

For support while writing about your shadow self:
- Always give us your best work.
- Share all of yourself in your written words.
- Post positive quotes on the wall in front of you when you're writing.
- Stay above the fray when you write. Go deep when you reflect.

Believe your writing will be cathartic for you

- Be courageous in your writing.
- See where "no guts no glory" applies to setting yourself free.
- Bring suspense and surprise to your stories.

Balance your emotions with detail

- Don't be so dramatic you leave out critical details to the story.
- Allow your readers to stay with you by speaking *to* them and not *over* them.
- Be sure you deliver.
- Give them a reason to tell a friend about your book.
- Make your words powerful. Give us the most important moments.
- Be willing to edit your work.
- Leave out unnecessary backstory to strengthen your work.

With the last memoir, *Sick as My Secrets*, I wrote and rewrote each chapter four or five times. Then my critique group looked at them. I used a lot of their suggestions before editing the chapters again. After that, I engaged a proofreader. I then hired a professional editor as my ultimate step. We did three rounds of edits. I thought it imperative a professional editor read my manuscript so I could be completely confident and proud of my efforts.

Readers want to cheer for you, take your journey, and ride your train. So, choose whichever moments you deem will be important to the reader. Imbue those moments with the power of your belief through your descriptions and word choices.

Go to great lengths to be authentic

- Travel to your hometown, a place you used to live or do business, or a faraway place, if that's what it takes to be authentic.
- Act to be authentic by personally writing letters or making phone calls for verification.
- Do whatever it takes to evoke memories by using the pictures, articles, and information you accumulate.
- Feel the feelings again. See the scenes and hear the voices.

I dedicated my book, *Sick as My Secrets*, to my friend Charm, who died in a horrendous car accident at the hands of a drunk driver. I extensively researched her death, the accident, and her burial with the police report and newspaper articles. The research contained information completely new to me. She was killed almost fifty years ago. I think of her every Fourth of July weekend and have for my entire adult life.

Discover more of who you are

- Be insightful with all of your writing.
- Avoid just filling a page.
- Read your work first as the owner of the story to claim it, hear your voice, and observe your style.
- Read your work as the reader of the story.
- Polish it for detail and emotion.
- Tell it like it is, bring your emotions to the surface, and show us who you are.
- Write often and revise even more to get to the heart of what you want to write and who you are as an author.

If you take yourself to task on anything that hits you as not authentic, if you follow your gut, your intuition, you will be the winner. You will succeed in getting to the truth, and so will your readers.

Although I found writing certain accounts difficult, it felt healing for me to do it. The benefits of stronger relationships with your readers and a clearer perception of what you want to write about makes for a cathartic experience. An enhanced energy about what you deem important to write emerges, along with the maturity to recognize it, leads to greater creativity.

Activity: Write about a topic you like

- Select a fun "how to" topic you can write about freely.
- Cover specific material and come to a clear understanding of the topic.
- Visualize your narrative and story, the numbers, bullets, and diagrams.
- Share your work with a reliable source in your writing circle.
- Be open to constructive criticism.

5. Transformation

We must always change, renew, or rejuvenate ourselves; otherwise, we harden.

— Johann Van Goethe, German writer and statesman

Be receptive to your subconscious ideas

To be fully happy and free with your writing, always allow yourself to transform as many times as you need to. Transformation isn't a future event—it is a present-day activity, a journey without a destination that grows with each new project. Change is inevitable as a writer. Transformation is by conscious choice as you become more confident and capable as an author.

As you write, ask these questions of yourself:

Why or how have you changed?

- Have you let go of being a perfectionist?
- Are you more carefree and open with your writing than before?

I no longer worry about what I look like on paper. I write from my heart and soul in each of my memoirs. I recommend that attitude to all those who write memoirs. I'm adamant about exposing vulnerability in my memoirs to endear myself to my readers. You must be bold.

What made that change happen or not happen for you?

- Was it the focal point of your book?
- Was it the crest, the turning point, of the story?
- Will the reader see the structure of the book as it is read?
- Does your format for the chapter work for the reader?

I shared my innermost thoughts to process many personal events. For me, these concerned traumatic experiences such as my sister's lung cancer noted in my first book, my issue with domestic violence and love addiction in the second memoir, and my alcoholism and recovery in my third memoir. Whatever it is, acknowledge and write about it.

What behaviors and decisions impacted your story?

- Did good and bad decisions impact your story?
- How were the painful times told effectively in your writing?

In my books, you'll read about the trauma I endured to learn some hard life lessons. People read memoirs to find those connections. In some ways, my memoirs read like a diary with the hope they will resonate with readers. Although some may not relate to all my experiences, those readers may know someone who could relate, or they may empathize with what I experienced.

Who and what played a part in your transformation?

- Was it by revealing the deeper elements of your story, the down and dirty, what really transpired?
- Was it coming clean and getting honest with those in your life?

You do best by humanizing your stories, speaking from the heart, and not holding back. I no longer concern myself with what others think. I feel no shame or guilt about my stories. I won't cheat myself or my writing with negative self-talk or negativity from someone else. Because of this, my life is more enjoyable and should be for the reader.

Be open to the wisdom coming to you

- Do you look at everything you've learned in a positive light?
- Do you genuinely bare your soul to tell your stories?
- Is your goal to be authentic always?
- Do you attempt to relay this attitude to the reader?

I look at myself in my journal reflections, and in my prayer and meditation practice, to make my memoirs memorable and interesting. If I had not told you about going to jail in my recovery story, I would not have given you the depth of what I had to do to accept my life changes. If I had not talked to you about the assault and anger in my love-addicted relationship, I would have cheated you out of what that really meant to me in my second memoir. I encourage you, my fellow memoir writers, to look at things in a positive light.

- Can you analyze the good and the challenging things you have experienced?
- Do you see the scenes in your mind's eye?
- Do you write in your journal, outline what you remember, then seek all the additional research?

By continually immersing yourself completely in the experiences you've been through, you can author your stories. You must be present so the reader can be too.

Consider the writing ideas and wisdom of other authors

Search for what works from your analysis and research:
- Take time to determine what you will share and what is too much.
- Focus on compelling narrative with all your words and the descriptions of your scenes.
- Understand what it means to go deep, to soul search.
- Don't be afraid to write what needs to be written to tell the story.
- Be subtle for effect, but don't leave out the parts that make the pages turn.
- Let the story speak for itself.
- Do not be in total control of the story.
- Speak from your heart and soul and write freely so the wisdom you have gleaned from life, and the ideas that come from your subconscious, show through your words.
- Don't rant about anything no matter how strongly you feel.

With my advocacy and books, I strive to move others to act too. My stories become a channel to create awareness of how society represents women who experience domestic violence and alcoholism. They allow my readers to freely speak out.

Be willing to share your life changes and turning points

Can you list them and categorize them?
- Do not be verbose. Be relevant to the times and the topics.
- Remember, memoir is not your life history. It is the time framework of an experience, success, or struggle.
- Recognize that brevity works only after enough details awaken understanding.

My recovery story started with my drinking experience. I then ushered the reader into the journey of how an innocent afternoon experience grew out of hand and eventually encompassed my life. I wanted to make a point. This is what addiction is all about. By starting from the beginning, I allowed the reader to come to their own conclusions on my handling of things, good and bad, and what they might do for themselves, a friend, or a family member.

Will you relate the life changes to your stories?

- Relate your story to the reader's story. Be human, real, brutally honest, and authentic.
- Give examples about that part of your life in descriptive, even graphic, scenes.

Initially, I met my purpose to help others by sharing with a therapist or a recovery sponsor. I then created my stories for the reader, including ideas and solutions. That is the mantra for my books, the premise of my writings. Nothing is more frustrating for the reader than to feel they are on the outside looking in on a situation they cannot relate to in any way.

Will you overlook any of your life changes?

- Understand your audiences through your emotions.
- Give the reader a reason to care about your memoir.

If they don't relate in the first few chapters, they'll miss the hook. They will have a tough time finding the crest of the story or how it resolves. You need that initial connection to communicate how you turned your life around. They will not experience the hope, feel the inspiration, or share your story with anyone else if they do not resonate with what you shared.

Do you recognize the hook and the crest as part of your transformation?

- Pique their empathy.
- Use detailed quotes or excerpts to enhance your stories.
- Relate the stories to the theme and threads of the book.
- Take them on a different journey.

Once I drew them into my stories of recovery, domestic violence survival, or love addiction, I made my nonfiction work available for scrutiny. By not letting my ego get in the way, and letting my soul shine, I secured my readers. By not boasting or being defensive, I helped them follow me to the solution.

Be aware of what happens throughout the arc of your story

Do you read your work aloud to know your story?

- Read your work aloud at least twice before an editor sees it.
- Write concrete notes if anything does not sound the way you intended it to sound.
- Work on any area that does not read well.

Reading memoir and nonfiction books aloud gives me immense pleasure. I spend much of my time drafting, promoting, or reading a book. I enjoy these activities and find them useful because nonfiction sheds light on the authors' voices. This habit feels quite natural.

Write the Memoir You're Afraid to Write

Do you ask yourself or others a lot of questions?

- Interview yourself with prepared questions before writing any of your stories.
- Write out the questions to prepare for an interview.
- Anticipate your critique group or proofreader's questions.
- Generate writing prompts the next day in your journal.

I am always ready for the positive editor and the negative critic in my head. By writing out answers to the questions that arise, I work outside of them and generate new thoughts and fresh ideas on my work.

Do you include the before and after?

- Establish the before and after as you write the peak of the story.
- Be flexible about where you close the story.
- Be sure you rework the peak moment many times to create the punch required to carry the reader through to the end.

A memoir contains several endings. You're writing about an experience or a time in your life. It comprises the before, the setup, and the after, which is the resolve. Those parts can be lengthy or short, depending on the topic and theme. By writing several ending scenes, you can determine the best one.

Did you analyze how others affected you?

- Dissect the final analysis, the critical evaluation of what happened to you, and what you are willing to share.
- Do not take the reader to the peak of the story and then drop them unprepared into the last half of the story.

- Do not leave them hanging for the duration of the story.
- Allow the reader to see the peak moment as the pinnacle and know things will start to happen, either for the better, or the inevitable.
- Be different. Be resolved to find the optimum solution.

This is the time in your story when you take a hard look at how you were affected. Be conscientious. Some real soul searching on how you lived your life, and how you could have lived it differently, is paramount to the story's ending. It is crucial to share the conclusions you drew or the lessons you learned from these experiences in the final manuscript.

Be honest with us about where it was painful and heart wrenching

Are you willing to be humble and truthful?

- Do not fear failure or success.
- Remember, you tell your stories truthfully to the best of your ability.
- Don't edit the outline, edit the work.
- Write with fierce abandon as if it's the first time you have gone down this road.
- Do a temporary table of contents (TOC) to line up your ideas and structure the memoir.
- Outline your work alongside your journaling, even if you do not use it all in your memoir.

Because you know your material, you are doing things correctly. It is your story and your truth. Humility goes a long way. Nobody is perfect. You can reach past the pain by preparing a casual outline to organize your thoughts. You can move the TOC order around. Right and wrong are nonexistent for memoirs, so you can't make a mistake. You can start at the end, the middle, or the beginning. Just start.

The mind map, or sketch, diagrams where you're going. Draw your map like a tree with a solid trunk, branches, and leaves. You use the tree's trunk as the core idea in the center. The main branches represent the threads of your theme, and the leaves clarify your threads' ideas. The painful and heart-wrenching parts will come as you remember your stories. They spread out and grow the tree from your subconscious to your heart to your pen.

Will you endear yourself to your readers?

- Go deep to the core of your being and let the magic happen.
- Do not hold back.
- Be willing to tell it all, or as much as you are comfortable with, and then a little more.

As we say in yoga, "Go to your edge." My memoirs go to my edge. I disclose truly deep emotions in the scenes. My *Sick as My Secrets* memoir is a notable example of that practice. The reader climbs into my head through a descriptive scene they can relate to at that time. I reveal my heart and soul, what is really going on, by including sidebars about each step of the way in my decades-long recovery. I capture the essence of what I am about for the reader through my innermost thoughts.

Be vulnerable and show your funny side

- Can you add a little self-deprecating humor?
- Don't be afraid to poke fun at yourself.
- Believe you have something to offer and forge ahead.

Even in the worst of times, I admitted I did something stupid and learned from it by being vulnerable. In other instances, I was egotistical and paid for it later. In my last memoir about my recovery journey, my self-deprecating humor took me a long way to accepting what happened to me. Humor helped me work through the chaos of the story so I could be of service to my readers looking for answers to similar instances. I could draft my stories without fear, shame, or guilt for anything I had done. I also wrote about gratitude and forgiveness to show where the healing took place.

Are you willing to learn about humor and research those who use it well?
- Don't fear the successful use of humor in memoirs.
- Research and read the works of several authors who use humor.
- Avoid feeling jealous of other authors who have successfully used humor.

I found using humor helpful to me and my readers. I did not hold back showing my funny side. Anticipate the reader's expectations and relate to them often to create their immediate consideration. The harder you work to be free, the luckier you will be with your reader's acceptance.

Be captivating and make your words fascinating

Can you think suspense and surprise, and understand the difference?
- Don't let your internal critic dictate where you will surprise the reader or what areas of suspense you will use.
- Put yourself completely back into those scenes and let them play out for your audiences.
- Know when surprise is enough or appropriate, or when the buildup of suspense will work better.
- Write, rewrite, and read aloud to refine what you have written.

My first suggestion? Read more memoirs for ideas and look for their surprise and suspense. You will not copy anyone's work. You will enhance yours with more knowledge and expertise.

Are you sure your vocabulary is real?
- Think through every sentence in the first round of edits.
- Write the section again and change up your words where needed.
- Enjoy the editing, then let the first draft go.
- Revise repeatedly until you can feel the words come alive.
- Be cautious of the words you choose, to make sense.
- Captivate the audience but don't turn them off by trying to impress them.

You don't need lofty words to make your point or tell your story. When you add beauty to your stories with exceptional words, you entertain and inform the reader, regardless of the genre. By focusing on building my vocabulary through revisions, my work improves.

Will you have a proofreader tell you where the wrong words are in the stories?
- Ask your critique group or writing partner to read your work aloud the second time through.
- Check to be sure the sound of your word choices resonates with your voice.
- Honor your style so the words will not leave the story flat.
- Don't think too hard about the feedback.
- Keep moving forward by adjusting what you wrote.
- Take notes as you go along with your critique group.
- Discuss your work with your proofreader later.

- Don't procrastinate when it is time to scratch or change a word.
- Keep revising.

By involving others early on with your work, you produce a more professional piece. There is no harm in having many eyes on your manuscript before it reaches an editor. You will decide in the end what works best for you. Be open to all these options.

Can you identify the correct words for your scenes?

- Be willing to accept suggestions.
- Develop a process when you edit so you can catch your overuse of a word and your repetitions.
- Make critiquing work for you by learning this skill.
- Set aside chunks of time for revisions, at least one or two hours at a time, to get into the flow of your process.
- Reread what you have done for at least thirty minutes.

Create a writing schedule that includes deadlines with your editor or proofreaders. Track what you're doing and mark your weak spots accordingly. You will be ready with notes the next time you meet if you continue to document every step of the way.

According to The Oxford English Dictionary, transformation is a thorough or dramatic change in form or appearance. This applies to you and your manuscript as much as it applies to life. Your work's metamorphosis is critical to your success and should be given plenty of attention at each step of the writing and editing process. All this effort corresponds to an important event in your life. Publishing a book, your memoir, for the first time or the third, is one of those times. It transforms your life.

Write the Memoir You're Afraid to Write

Activity

1. Write a short (two or three pages) account of a life change you acknowledge.
2. Use any part of your timeline.
3. Allow your imagination to flow freely and don't share with anyone.
4. Don't edit and write nonstop for at least fifteen minutes.
5. Come back to it the next day to reference the transformation.
6. Capture the lesson you learned and go forward.

6. Themes and Threads

In every bit of honest writing in the world, there is a base theme. Try to understand men. If you understand each other, you will be kind to each other. Knowing a man well never leads to hate and always leads to love.

—John Steinbeck, American author

The theme of your memoir is your central topic, the underlying message or big idea. With it, the author tries to convey a critical belief about life to their readers, usually through something universal in the message, a lesson, or the moral of the story. The author can divide it into a couple of categories: the reader's concept of the topic, or the work's statement about the topic.

The threads running through the theme and the memoir illustrate the many parts of the story and highlight the characters through various scenes. Your threads clarify and tell the story.

The deep thread of your memoir

The deep thread of your memoir focuses on one event that changed everything for you. It may be an experience you survived or endured, which made you a better person in the end. It made you a healthier, stronger, or more resilient person whom others want to emulate as they read your words.

It's that lesson you've learned which you must share. You've come out on the other side and feel a calling to tell the story. When compelled to do so, you can be of help to others in a big way. Finally, it can be a universal truth you know to be true or a situation you've experienced and deemed inspiring to others. It can be all the above.

Once you determine the focus, the deep thread, of your memoir, and recognize it, you're ready to weave all your threads into the story. You'll find your threads by mind-mapping: sketching or diagraming your theme. Through this process, you can put your thoughts in order. Mind-mapping is a brainstorming process with focus at its core. These threads, the branches of the tree trunk, will help you build and grow your story. They contain leaves too, so you can continue to break down your story.

Throwing away past perfectionism allows mind-mapping to flow. What God intended me to write comes forth. I see the theme I want and the threads I need to complete it.

I am now comfortable with who I am. My writing is alive with my truth and my storytelling. I am proud of the stories that came forth from this process and can now help others with issues such as grief, love addiction, domestic violence relationships, and alcoholism. My age enriches my words. I've grown as a writer and share a universal truth I know today: forgiveness has power.

Threads in your memoir relate to your experience

By looking earnestly at the following areas, by connecting your theme and threads, your scenes will extend your stories. Evaluate each of these intently:
- Childhood: family and friends
- Adolescence: dreams and fears
- Young adulthood: goals and aspirations
- Early adulthood: career and family
- Later adulthood: senior living and retirement
- Legacy: accomplishments and regrets

I choose a peaceful writer's life. Reviewing my life in stages is critical to my overall happiness. My best creativity surfaces when I have the courage to ignore what others think and simply write. My threads emerge when I take emotional risks with my writing by examining these lifeline categories. My experiences benefit the reader with hope and inspiration.

Your threads connect to your theme

Examine your threads from all angles:
- Evaluate if your threads relate directly to your theme.
- Match the mind-mapping you have experienced.
- Determine which threads are the most important to your memoir.
- Take them one by one and visualize them in your scenes.
- Personalize them and bring them back around to your theme.
- Identify the threads in your theme and spark your memory.

Look at your threads from all angles and be sure you have not missed a vital nugget to the story, one you may be subconsciously eliminating:
- Interviews: friends and family
- Photos, music, and videos: old and new
- Letters: yours and others
- Outlines: make for each chapter
- Journals: keep now and then
- Documents and records: analyze legal and family

My memoirs are both different and connected. They cover various aspects of my themes at distinct times. All of them stem from an outline, journal writing, and research into important records. All of their content—grief and loss, difficult relationships, and addiction and recovery—overlap and challenge the reader. Though heart-wrenchingly honest and cathartic for me to write, I designed their themes to help people.

The details of it

To get to the details, "the nuts and bolts" of writing to the memoir's theme, find the threads and dissect your writing. For example, the recovery theme in *Sick as My Secrets* uses threads to show what happened, why it happened, when the reckoning happened, what comes after acceptance and rehabilitation, and more.

You need to take a couple of basic steps:
- Stay in your chair and write.
- Have a designated writing space and time.
- Be committed to those times and that space.
- Believe writer's block is a myth and look forward to writing.

Next to my computer, I keep a rock that says, *"Just Write."* In our condominium, we have dedicated an office to writing, with space for two desks, my laptop computer, three bookshelves, and anything else to make it my space. The printer, additional shelving, credenza, inspirational wall photos, and live plants signify I've reserved this space for working, writing, or promoting my books. I know what I am going to do there, for that designated amount of time. It is conducive to writing.

Find your space and do these things to keep it ready:
- Do not answer emails or hit the spell check.
- Don't text, message, or answer the phone.
- Never bring food to the room.
- Always keep your chapter theme in mind.
- Write with fierce abandon.
- Allow the threads to reveal themselves.

After writing for a certain length of time, enjoy a snack somewhere else in your home or take a walk. Be conscious of staying organized and disciplined to allow your brain to work for you and for the muse to appear.

Before you begin, I recommend you organize your desk and put a few things away to give yourself a clean space without distraction. Once done, write notes in a journal or some other log. Outline often while thinking about your writing. You might do more research before you begin your first draft, or even a second draft. All the threads related to the theme may not surface in the first or second round of writing or research. It may take several drafts and mind-mapping to show the core, the theme, and the threads. The concept begins to develop by taking time before each chapter starts to unfold.

Before you begin to write, make a list of which tactics work for you. Develop a plan that is comfortable and productive for you. Add to it as you go along and remove the clutter. Claim your time and place to write.

Write the way you talk

During my years as a realtor, I learned that writing home contracts with an authentic voice was critical. We were told to speak and write to be understood, to communicate well, and to not try to impress. This philosophy applies now in my writing career. I work to be easily understood and clear on the page, but at a higher standard than casual speaking. It's about the readers.

Writing in a clear and genuine voice helps people comprehend your story, ideas, and perspective. They will want to listen and read more. This type of voice sells your book. Your ability to inspire is due to your meaningful content.

I especially focused on this in *Gifts of Sisterhood*, where I took emotional risks to connect with women on the topic of grief using an authentic and clear voice for those who knew and loved my sister.

Using your own words, even your vernacular on occasion, endears people to you. By reading aloud your second draft, you'll hear what you're saying, catch errors, and feel much of what the reader will feel. By recreating the lessons you've learned in your scenes, you will bring the scenes alive. Visualize your scenes every step of the way. The readers will recognize quickly if your voice is sincere.

I published *Three Husbands and a Thousand Boyfriends* in 2016. I shared stories about surviving in a domestic violence relationship including an assault. By expressing myself well and describing what happened to me during those brutal experiences, I healed. I chose words critical to the message's success. At reading and signing events, I share my courage with my readers in honest words and a heartfelt voice.

The way you talk portrays your writing's emotional beats, an important aspect as well. You may change your voice inflection at stops along your path to reflect a shift in emotion and emphasize a point. If you are authentic, your voice stays true to form. It enhances the conversation in your dialogue and message in your scenes.

Emotional beats are critical in these ways:
- They validate your story.
- They make it real for the reader.
- They document your life.
- They enhance the experience of your adventures.
- They bring forth what is entertaining, educational, or informative.

One way to stay with your flow each day is to have a trick to start the next day. You leave a teaser at the end of the page, such as a provocative question. That way you'll be curious to start again. When you write the way you talk, you don't perpetuate your life myth about who you are supposed to be. The reader receives the real story, and your voice is spot-on and unique. They'll identify with you. Do not copy anyone. Using others' work for inspiration is good, but give readers the real you.

By using my God-given talent as a writer helping others, I continue to preside over a women's writers' group to gain knowledge and nurture friendships. Through appreciating our writing opportunities, we find camaraderie. The talks I give to the community, law enforcement, students, business organizations, and church groups are well received because they experience my truth. I feel strongly about women's rights and how grief, loss, and trauma have touched my life. They motivate me to give back. When the audience member relates to my story, the purpose of the story is complete.

Write the Memoir You're Afraid to Write

Being a workshop presenter, sharing my wisdom, insight, expertise, and knowledge, is paramount to my legacy. With my latest memoir, *Sick as My Secrets*, I moved forward into another productive phase of my life. My finest work appears by openly sharing my almost forty years of recovery from alcoholism.

Make your story come alive

To make readers fully experience your story, you must take chances and risks and draft the story you are afraid to write. By building the story and unlocking your truth, you tell your story authentically, without embellishment. You might enhance what is foggy in your memory, only taking creative license when you're sure it is for the right reason.

Believing truth is better than fiction, you will write your best work with the following:

- Be provocative and put yourself out there.
- Give them all you have.
- Don't leave the theme threadbare.
- Put all your truth on the table.
- Wind the thread back to the beginning to give us the full story.
- Do not cheat the reader of vital details.
- Author the book you want to find on a bookshelf.
- Let it be the one that captivates and keeps the reader wanting more.

Persistence is a critical factor in achieving anything. I do not give up, but regroup, revamp, and redefine my book business and writing projects each year. When a writing opportunity comes, it is God's plan for me. By being flexible in my writing life, I can help other writers. By learning to share the wisdom of experience, I see my true gift to others.

Find the heart of your scenes

Keep digging deeper and deeper with each rewrite to clarify what your threads are and how they define your theme. Be increasingly specific with each revision so you can feel your heartbeat and hear your voice clearly. Remember, this is a memoir. This is your truth. You are not writing for a newspaper. You are writing to connect with your readers at a deeper level.

Keep asking yourself these important questions:

- Did I allow my mind to run free and capture my true story?
- Did I give myself permission to draft my story uncensored?
- Did I keep writing until there was nothing left and I was exhausted?
- Did I recreate my memories, no matter what they were?
- Did I trust that whatever came to mind needed to be written about in some form?
- Did I write with fierce abandon?

Coming from a generation of idealists, my soul needs to give back. With that in mind, I meticulously draft my scenes at the heart of the story and don't leave anything out. Building a foundation for women to pursue their writing with my own example of free writing rewards me immensely.

My generation of post-WWII babies is often stereotyped as self-indulgent. We write and recreate to redefine our lives. We have a lot to write about, and a new wave of creativity and activism emerges. Writing with fierce abandon is what we do.

Every scene has a purpose

If the purpose of the scene is not visible, find it and immediately add what is necessary. You do not want to lose your reader.

- Ask yourself, "What is missing?"
- Address what to do to find what is missing.
- Do not hold back.
- Write toward a spellbinding story.
- Bring them into the scene so they can visualize what is happening.
- Help them identify with you.
- Do not cheat the reader of conflict. Move the story along.
- Take time to reel them in.

This leads to solutions and a conclusive ending. The conflict gives the book purpose, adds spice to the story, provides the narrative's turning point, and even creates the story's joy.

Now that you've emptied your head and are free to write, establish categories for your life. Be assured, we all have conflict. Let your mind give you the topics that belong in your memoir, especially the conflicts. The reader is looking to you to create some order from your chaos, to solve the mysteries, and to resist judging yourself for having conflict.

Listen for the answers and they will come, even if that's not what you did years ago. You can give us the solution in retrospect. We're looking to you for guidance.

Tell your story in an intriguing way by doing the following:

- Read your list of categories often as you write.
- Be willing to write on all categories.
- Discard a chapter if necessary.
- Align your categories with age, location, or people.
- Outline each category first on a separate paper.
- Study it intently for content.

- Use your style to put your entire self behind the book.
- "Just write" like you have never written before.
- Do not look back or stop.
- Do not hit the spellcheck too often.

The threads will weave themselves once you let your theme come alive.

I have things to create, words to write, and voices to share. I am comfortable at this age, so I can allow myself to share my life in memoirs highlighting the themes and threads that take me there. I offer my best to my readers as I continue writing and sharing enthusiastically. My readers look for the raw truth in my work. I give them what they want and show the heart of writing memoir.

Activity: Act!

1. Select eight to ten photos you may use later in your memoir.
2. Place them near three-by-five cards.
3. Ponder an action or dialogue for everyone and write them on the cards.
4. Set the photos up in a sequence to show the action.
5. Keep your speech brief. Think a lot about making a point.
6. Visualize your actions to bring them to life.
7. Keep it fun and free and don't labor on it.
8. Use your findings to start or continue your writing

7. Necessities

Facts are stubborn things; and whatever may be our wishes, our inclinations, or the dictates of our passions, they cannot alter the state of the facts and evidence.

— John Adams, second U.S. president

To write demands certain necessities and commitments indispensable to your success. Pacing yourself, resisting binge writing when you know you should stop, and preparing for the next day, for sure. Additionally, you need a trusted reader, a friend or partner, who can ensure you possess the time to write undisturbed.

Here are a few more necessities to contemplate:

Present tense, past tense, or both?

Write portions of your book as it flows, and then decide on the tense. This is your story and your voice. You are the storyteller. In today's world of writing, a crossover in tense works if it is done correctly, within a chapter, not a paragraph.

You may like both the past and present versions. Give the process time. Be willing to try both or just stick with one. Remember this is your writing life.

You are at the helm. Eventually you will have other eyes on your work: a proofreader, often a critique group, and certainly an editor. In the end, look to add flair and style to your voice.

Dialogue is necessary

I cannot urge you enough to include dialogue in your memoir writing. Dialogue places readers in action, a necessity when writing memoirs. It makes a story come alive and brings *you* to the scenes and your readers. Dialogue helps readers stay in the moment and truly hear the author's voice. You know what the person might say, so say it.

Dialogue may not come easily to you. Reading dialogue aloud from other memoirs can be extremely helpful to a writer. The key: visualize the action. Practice makes perfect, and sometimes less is more. It is so easy to make sentences too long, which is not the way you talk.

Beware of using too much dialogue, however. You don't want the reader to start skimming through it. Narrative is critical to stories in memoir, and combining the two makes for an enjoyable read. Balance to move the story along.

Facts add to the story

With more than enough research, you can create details for the story. Some suggestions:

- Research plenty of backstory and information to consider.
- Be specific and descriptive with your draft without depending only on adjectives.
- Work with visualization by speaking aloud and mentally reliving the scene.
- Do not lose the details. Pay attention to them.
- Identify the trivial things about any person critical to the story.
- Be honest about the details since exaggerating them will be obvious.
- Don't vary your truth with unnecessary facts.

Movies written about memoirs or based on true stories often succeed. The memoir genre is on the rise in all mediums.

Many people see real-life stories as more interesting and inspiring than fiction.

Raise your story with action

When you elevate your story with action, the reader believes you will eventually resolve the story's conflict. It may not be obvious but that is the fun of reading. All memoirs need a resolution. Your reader is looking for a solution. They want to see you come out the other end, unscathed, and as a success in your own way. They want to learn from your lessons.

Some points to remember:

- Make resolutions happen with clear concepts.
- Build your memoir into a page-turner by not holding back.
- Use staccato sentences often, especially in many of the critical scenes.
- Don't allow the reader to become bored and put your book down.

Make an impression

You get one shot to make a good impression with your content. In the scenes, something must happen, and it must happen early, or your reader is on to another book.

So, make these ideas a part of your writing life:
- Let the writing happen as freefall expressions from your memory.
- Think about "hotspots" to punctuate the writing.
- Write with fierce abandon. Edit later.
- Enjoy your second and third drafts.
- Let your words hit the paper quickly in the first draft.
- Don't think too much.

- Do put things in chronological order for an outline.
- Be willing to change your mind.

Readers want your stories. And they expect the manuscript structure and format to be clear. They do not want to find your errors or missing parts. They want to know you gave five or six unbiased people a look at your third draft.

With that in mind, remember to:
- Write passionately from your heart and soul.
- Focus on what is important to you, regardless of the feedback you receive.
- Make your manuscript for you first and your readers' appreciation second.
- Deal with death and other challenges so they don't haunt you later.

This writing will be cathartic and healing for you in several ways. We are all different, and you will find space. When you see and feel the difference, you will grow with your revisions and get to know yourself and others better through your drafts.

Structure the book to drive storylines

When you research other memoirs, you glean ideas for many things, including your book's structure. Their ways may not be your way but are worth consideration.

Work to apply the following:
- Read other memoirs when you write to keep your creativity flowing.
- Take notes on what you read and continue writing in your journal.
- Remember to place the characters and the scenes in your story's era, time, and place.
- Use trivia if it pertains to the story, such as music, food, clothes, and cars.
- Don't let the scenes drag or the trivia bog you down.

Write the Memoir You're Afraid to Write

- Do not hurt the book by filling up your story with unnecessary details.
- Make the time clock clear in each chapter.
- If you are not sure of a person's name or another feature from the era, confirm it.

When readers see dates, they set the clock with the clothes of the era, the movies, the songs, and the events you've offered. Weaving such elements throughout your story will keep your reader until the end. You may find this challenging, but it is so necessary to build the structure of your book.

- Don't forget the theme and threads of your stories.
- Refer to the threads often to stay organized around the main theme running through the book.

By adding the "frosting on the cake" and making your book worth a read, you tell your story well.

The following helps you make connections to your readers, capture the essence of your memoir, and develop a full-bodied story:

- Write because you must write and vividly tell your stories.
- Do not think about how hard it is or how much work it is to do correctly.
- Forget about how much competition exists in the book industry and just write.
- Reward yourself for doing the challenging work and making the book better.
- Surround yourself with supportive people as you write.
- Join a face-to-face or online writing community.
- Do not stop creating.
- Tell your stories in detail. Your readers need to hear them unchained.

When you understand your purpose, your theme, and what the memoir is about, you're ready to wrap up your memoir concept. This will take time and a lot of finesse. You will not fear how many other memoirs grace the market when you visualize yourself proudly presenting yours to the world.

Activity: Guess Who?

1. Select four to six pictures of people, unknown to you, from a magazine.
2. Separately, write a quick description of each person in a clear and detailed manner.
3. Share the pictures and descriptions with your writing partner or critique group.
4. Don't tell them which picture belongs to which description.
5. Have them try to match the descriptions with your pictures.
6. Later, share your answers with them and discuss the results.

8. "Waste" Time Creating

God made time, but man made haste.
— Irish proverb

The phrase "wasting time" takes you to thoughts of, "I need to get up earlier," or "I need to do more." You start trying to figure out how you can find those extra minutes. You ask yourself what you're doing that someone else might do for you.

In this chapter, you are not going to focus on to-do lists or overestimate what you can achieve. You are not going to overload yourself or say "should." But, most of all, you will not stress out about finishing your book. What you are going to do is support yourself.

Wastefulness

Waste a little time contemplating your situation before you start to write, while you're writing, and after you've written your final draft. Doing this is a favor to your book and yourself as an author.

Try to:
- Germinate your main ideas by thinking everything through several times.
- Take deep breaths with every idea.

- Detach yourself from how much time it will take to reach your objectives.
- Allow yourself time to create the end of this process in your mind's eye. This is your emotional amplifier, visualizing it without seeing it with your eyes.

Next, work mentally on the complimentary tasks to make these objectives happen, such as strong dialogue, scene descriptions, and structure. Finally, focus on how they will work with your writing journey. Imagine all this happening at a comfortable pace.

- Don't confuse your efforts with the results that will come.
- Don't confine yourself to a limited time slot.
- Give this writing a chance to be your best work.
- Honor your life's work, your story.

All of this takes time, a lot of time, time you have, time you deserve. An old adage says: "Why is there never enough time to do it right and always enough time to do it over?"

For many years, I had a refrigerator magnet with that saying on it. After a party at my townhouse, I noticed it had disappeared. Somebody must have needed it badly to remove it. I didn't replace the sign with the anonymous quote but forged it into my memory.

Tracking

To add to your writing, do the following:
- Write down how much time you estimate it will take to research a new topic.
- Outline a chapter or do a first edit of a rough draft.
- Do this on a regular basis, while serving as the keeper of your time.
- Ascribe value to this idea by prioritizing.

You're not being compensated for a project in a piecemeal manner. Do whatever it takes to complete the items listed above correctly, to the best of your ability.

I learned this in the real estate business. Once a client began looking for a home or entrusted me to list their home, I did whatever it took to bring the sale to fruition. If it meant long days, evening work, or weekends, I did it. Keeping track of the hours spent in research or analysis, as well as in negotiations, I did what needed to be done to make the result happen positively for everyone. I view the book business in the same way.

Although you often do the things mentioned, you can underestimate the time it takes to do them. Do you overestimate the time it takes you to clean up your home office, yet underestimate the time to prepare for a new week of writing?

I recommend the following:
- Be diligent, not confining, about your tracking.
- Take it seriously yet remain flexible.

Once you know how you spend your writing time, you will be more creative and not stifled by distractions. You cannot fully calculate your time when writing a memoir, especially when you need to go back to places from your past or conduct interviews. To free yourself to do these things, appreciate them as a matter of immense importance to your result.

My time spent researching my *Sick as My Secrets* memoir was consuming. I went back to both the criminal and the civil courts and spoke to the lawyers for both trials. I logged in a lot of time making copies, doing interviews, and reading material on the process. None of this effort was in vain since it took me into my scenes. I felt the experience again. Although I used little of the information, it put me in the right frame of mind. That's all part of research, of the backstory. Do what you need to do to glean your best material.

Prioritization

Use Post-it notes and make them work for you. Put them on the wall in front of your computer.

Dwight Eisenhower was the first to suggest the following categories I suggest you use:

- Urgent and Important. Example: Outline your next chapter to meet a deadline or call your editor.
- Not Urgent but Important. Example: Research your target audience or future marketing steps.
- Urgent but Not Important. Example: Check the sales at an office store for supplies or read material.
- Neither Urgent Nor Important. Example: Read *The New York Times* book reviews or browse Amazon.

The goal is to go light on the "Urgent and Important" area. Please don't stress and cheat yourself out of a wonderful day of writing and creating. Your comfort zone is in the "Not Urgent but Important" area. Here, you can be the most productive and eventually the most creative. The others will take care of themselves in time.

Scheduling

Hoping for the best isn't a plan. Treat your writing life as a career, not a job or a hobby. Follow a schedule for appointments with yourself and those in your writing circle.

My book production team consists of a cover designer, an editor, a book layout and design person, my critique group, a writing partner (proofreader/author/husband), and many others. I'm cognizant of what needs attention. I give my time where needed yet know when to step away to think and waste a little time daydreaming about how I'm going to accomplish my next task.

Complicated and/or busy doesn't equal better. If you take ten years to author your book versus five years, so be it. Your writing must be excellent. Quality counts, not quantity of time and effort.

The following considerations are critical:
- Clarify what is important to you.
- Ask yourself when your most productive time of the day is.

- Schedule other activities every day, such as exercise or lunch.
- Don't be afraid to change this after experimenting for ninety days.

This is your writing life and your chance to ramp up your creativity. Time is on your side. You can manage it, so waste a little now to benefit more later.

To create my best work, I am willing to waste time to be prepared, for research, thoughts, quiet time, and contemplation. I accomplish this by reading and taking notes on what I read. Anytime I feel the need, I go to my journal. I intuitively know now when I need to waste a little time talking to myself.

Gratification

The adage "procrastination is assassination" holds true here too. So:
- Get the challenging task done first and earlier each day.
- Delay gratification to avoid worry.
- Take that demanding task head-on, knowing you can get it done.
- Ask for help when needed.

I am always willing to waste time practicing, experimenting, and using trial and error to reach my writing goals. I am not afraid to go the extra mile. I know with significant risk comes great reward, and the truth I uncover will set me free. No pats on the back needed for me. I am on a mission when I write.

Document

At times, you grow busy and forget or miss appointments or deadlines. Not often, but you do.

To avoid this:
- Write items down or log them in on your phone.
- Practice this gift of positivity for yourself.

If you want to keep your creative juices flowing, you need to focus on the things at hand with your writing, despite everything else swirling around the writing process. If you are not staying on task and organized, you fall short.

You need these reminders, especially if writing is a new career or a new part of your busy life. Preferably, you will put it in a writing journal, on a legal pad, or on your phone or computer. Clear space for thinking and creativity to enter. Whatever you use, always be consistent and keep it with you.

I prefer to use my handwritten Day-Timer, which I have used for forty years, to plant commitments into my subconscious. I added my iPhone for backup and convenience. It's good practice to do it twice, to reinforce in my mind what I need and want to do. This way, I can disengage and forget about time and observe my surroundings. I let my mind wander. By doing this, I liberate my inner self to think and gain more creative thoughts.

Cheating

If you schedule your workout time or your morning walk for seven o'clock in the morning, exercise and relax without guilt. If you prefer lunch at eleven thirty in the morning because you are up by five thirty, enjoy it.

Make sure to:
- Schedule yourself by your clock.
- Value your time by working in two-to-three-hour increments.
- Be kind to your back by moving around.
- Find quiet alone time to replenish your soul.

What you physically write moves from your head to your heart to your soul. Your mind, body, and spirit are connected in your writing. Give yourself a chance to experience this phenomenon.

When I write as part of my morning meditation, I am not wasting my time but opening the door to my soul, my subconscious. Every minute I give myself allows my writing thoughts to come back to me tenfold.

You are the boss. This opportunity to write is a precious gift. Be loyal and steadfast.

Remember to:
- Respect yourself at all times in the process.
- Don't cheat yourself. Time to create is well spent.
- Change your schedule. It is not carved in stone.
- Treat your writing life like a diamond, not easily cut into a new shape.

Starting

A steady pace will energize your habit that strengthens as your creative juices and ideas flow. You will soon be in the swing of writing consistently. Wasting time by creatively scheming as you walk or enjoy a cup of tea in a quiet room is valid. Push past the tendency to put off until tomorrow what you can do today.

- Take small steps, then walk briskly. Move more quickly each time.
- Maintain a cheerful outlook to influence your behavior, and vice versa.
- Step outside yourself to see where you're going and keep moving.

I stopped writing my *Three Husbands and a Thousand Boyfriends* book at one point due to the demands of my consulting business, the writing group I manage, and my personal life obligations. I took almost six years to draft that book. The gap between my first book and my second book was longer than I had originally anticipated. Once I realized my choice to allow somebody else's time to run my life, I reflected on my situation. I avoided anger about the lost time; it was gone. I sat alone each day, present with my thoughts, and moved forward in twenty-four-hour increments. I finished that memoir a year later.

Value

All of your time counts. If you have an hour to spare in the morning before work or an appointment, focus on your writing. You can write a journal entry, do a little research, draft out a chapter, or reread yesterday's writing to prepare for the day. Value every minute.

If you arrive for an appointment fifteen minutes early, stay in your car or walk around the building. Think about what you wrote that morning or the day before.

- Make voice notes on your phone and allow the creative juices to flow to you.
- Seek the wandering mind. It's your wealth of information coming forward from your lifetime.
- Be open and aware of your surroundings.
- Make every moment a suitable time for writing by remaining open.

Online

Online apps exist for everything. If you're not organized by nature, or not someone who keeps lists or remembers easily, let your fingers do the walking. Document everything you can.

As mentioned earlier, I prefer to first use the Day-Timer book. I physically enter what I am doing with pen and paper. By doing that, I absolutely waste time and create too. I am more creative and productive because of that tried-and-true activity, with no fear of missing a creative idea that's come my way. At the end of the month, I re-read my writing journal notes for the past thirty days and check to see if my accomplishments match my goals. I transfer what remains to the next month.

My Day-Timer refills arrive every six months. I keep seven years of completed pages in storage for backup and refer to them often, especially for our tax preparation. They have saved me time and energy beyond measure. I journal in them, too, keep quotes, total daily expenses, track the weather, and log in my affirmations.

To stay on task and prioritize your writing project, turn away from your social media and blog posts. Allow your computer to be your friend, not your foe. You can access Day-Timer, and other programs like it, online to complement your phone apps.

Limits

Don't set limits on your writing and research, on your meditation and journal writing, or your "time-wasting periods" in the morning or later in the day. All are critical to your finished product and need a prominent level of importance.

You can:
- Prioritize each activity.
- Give yourself space every day to evaluate where you are with your writing.
- Honor the limits you've set and the space you've given yourself.
- Don't feel guilty about them.

Once you hit your limit in one area, move on to what else needs to be done, even if it is quiet time or errands.

Breaktime

Make plans with yourself for lunch, even if you're not in that habit. Something light. You'll find this critical to your success and well-being.
- Enjoy a leisurely meal, read something, and relax.
- Consider taking a short thirty-minute walk and enjoy a power bar or apple.
- Detach from your work to rejuvenate yourself.
- Play a game or do an activity at home or while out for a walk.

It is essential to stay healthy both physically and mentally. Writing, publishing, and marketing a book can be a grueling process, more so than you anticipated. It may be the hardest time, and the best time, of your life. A time ever loved.

I enjoy tennis. I play twice a week, on Friday morning in a women's league at the park, and on Tuesday morning with a group of neighbors. I play nine months out of the year here in Arizona. I also practice yoga as part of an intermediate class all year. These add a sense of calm to my writing life, a chance to draw away from writing to regroup. I chose these activities as a way to unplug and I rarely miss them. A break adds to my creativity.

Balance

You have a life away from writing. The title "writer" is not your identity. It is only a part of who you are today. By adding balance to create a well-rounded life and smelling the roses along the way, you will launch your book and connect with the audience. Your readers want to know you more, beyond what you wrote in your memoir.

These activities add balance to your writing life:
- See movies.
- Read books, especially memoirs.
- Spend leisurely time in galleries and at cultural events.
- Walk through the woods.

Disciplined, structured time is for your left-brain self, while your creative self, your right brain, seeks your frivolous self. You do not need to be driven all the time. When you think you're wasting time, you are not.

By embracing this philosophy, you will stay positive and motivated to finish your work and feel excited to promote it. Take all the time you need and write with fierce abandon to create the work you envision. You will finish your memoir.

Activity: Creating

1. Choose an odd, even unknown holiday or day celebrated during your childhood. An unpopular one triggers creativity best.
2. Plan a celebration for it. Include flyers, commercials, or an opening.
3. Describe in detail what happens at the celebration.
4. Be imaginative. Use illustrations or slogans.

9. Driving Ambition

Keep away from people who try to belittle your ambitions. Small people always do that, but the great ones make you feel that you, too, can become great.

— Mark Twain, American writer

Merriam-Webster defines ambition as "a strong desire to achieve something, typically requiring determination and hard work." Writers experience ambition as an inner desire to achieve success with writing, coupled with a belief we're doing it for the right reasons, knowing full well it may not be the key to financial success.

Career ambition

Career ambition is often seen as moving up from your current position to something else more desirable. In the writer's case, ambition might mean they realized their dream of publishing a book, drafted an award-winning article, or received an offer to write a movie script. These accomplishments can mean a lot.

This strong urge to accomplish your ambition is satisfied by one or more of the following:

- Learn all you can by attending national writing conferences.
- Hire professionals in editing, cover design, and book formatting.

- Understand all the options to publish your manuscript.
- Inform yourself on all the social media available for book promotion.

I started our publishing company, Brooks Goldmann Publishing Company, LLC, in part to satisfy my ambition. We independently publish our own books and those of other authors who seek consultation with us. This move expanded my "author's platform" as an authority on independent publishing. My reputation as an expert in the growing field of publishing established me as a point of reference. This offered me the opportunity to truly know what was going on in the world of books. I could stay ahead of this ruthless game called the book business.

Do you love to write? Do you hunger for recognition? Does your ambition grow from your writing? If you're a good writer, you'll naturally be ambitious. If you are a timid writer who isolates at home, you will need to nourish your ambition by communicating with other writers for encouragement.

Consider these questions:
- Do I see myself at a book launch?
- Am I elated at the idea of signing one of my books?
- Am I seeking recognition?
- Do I aspire to five-star reviews?

The book business is about succeeding, not just doing. You make it happen.
- Do not wait for it to happen.
- Learn all you can about the industry and apply what you learn.
- Define outcomes and set goals to achieve them.
- Achieve your long-term career ambition of becoming a published author.

Commit to your ambition by following these two concepts:

Use what drives your ambition to grow and push yourself as a writer.
- Don't just delve headlong into your writing.
- Take time to find out about yourself and your burning desires.
- Be sure you know where you are going and why you are going there.
- Use your writing plan and your outline as your guide.

Get uncomfortable, and do more than what you think is possible.
- Use reflection to know what really drives you in your writing.
- Take your writing seriously, not yourself.
- Use your journal writings to discover the clues that rise from your heart.
- Consider taking your writing in a completely different direction.

In my second memoir, *Three Husbands and a Thousand Boyfriends*, I initially wrote about post-traumatic stress (PTS). Still in the throes of PTS as the result of an assault, I wrote for a couple of years on the topic. I conducted a significant amount of research and analyzed whether the book's story and voice reflected my truth. Eventually, I realized PTS was not the focus of the book. I eliminated the chapters I wrote on my father's and cousin's wartime experiences. Although horrific stories in and of themselves, they were not my stories. My memoir had to be my PTS story woven into the main theme of love addiction and domestic violence and its impact on my intimate relationships.

Consider it an honor to have anyone read your work.
- Work to have influence on the lives of others.
- Carry a strong message of hope.

- Be inspirational.
- Give the reader a chance to absorb your message.

Be grateful and seek respect for writers, which includes you.
- Use your ambition to impact the lives of your readers.
- Leave a proud legacy.
- Recognize the theme and the threads important to your story.
- Tell your story truthfully.

No matter what theme you use in your memoir, what advocacy work you pursue, or what educational goal you set, your story will impact somebody or should not have been chosen.

Pure Unadulterated Ambition

Pure unadulterated ambition, an energy inside you, expects to be used. It liberates your passion for writing, your desire to tell your stories, and your longing to find success as an author. It launches your conviction about a topic you feel must get out there. You choose memoir to tell the truth about what you believe needs to be said.

The genre of memoir writing asks you to believe in writing for the greater good, have something valuable to say, and want to be a part of something bigger than you initially anticipated. You desire a greater experience in life than you previously longed for. In memoir, you choose to tell your stories regardless of obstacles.

As mentioned, I do advocacy work with addiction and domestic violence awareness groups and organizations. My last two books focus on my personal experience in these areas. As such, I have a platform to share my stories, to fulfill my mission of helping others, and to offer hope and inspiration. Public speaking and facilitating workshops are second nature for me and, for that, I am profoundly grateful. These presentations are a vehicle to communicate even more than what I have said in my books. Advocacy is an ambitious goal I've chosen for myself.

These ideas may sound new to you, or they may not. You'll find writers from many sectors in society, many of them timid. Then there are those of us, like me, who come to writing memoirs from a business background, a sales background, or a consulting and speaking background. I've spoken, written, and shared my stories for a long time.

We all have a particular asset within our ambition that will override any challenge we encounter. This personal asset might be a talent or a skill. The skills of writing can be learned through arduous work. Your hidden talent, necessary for your story, can be brought forth with encouragement and desire. Ambition leads to the triumph of your book in hand, the book signing, the book sales, and of course the pure joy of the journey to authorship.

Now that I'm blessed to have independently published three memoirs for myself, two additional books for my husband, and about three dozen memoir and nonfiction books for other authors, I can assure you of the special joy in this accomplishment. A pleasure even greater than when that first box of books arrives at your doorstep, or when the book shows up on Amazon.com and says, "Ready to Order." You will find a smile deep in your soul.

Once you've realized your dream of becoming a published author, your ambition transforms into your will to write, more than anything else. You will do whatever it takes to bring your book to fruition and find the courage to improve and do it again. You'll want to bring a story into the world, not just to "publish" or to say you've "published." Do it thoughtfully and with purpose, ensuring a quality product.

That type of ambition could carry you to do it a third time. This is how you find success in the writing world, by going the extra mile, choosing to give up other things, and unleashing sheer determination. Unfortunately, I have seen aspiring writers come and go in my critique group and in my writers' group. Some did not have this driving ambition. They did not make their writing goals a priority, whether out of fear, lack of financial help, or misguided ambition.

They did not have a burning desire to finish their book, no matter what it took. They knew they had an idea and a story to tell, but they became distracted, lacked enough motivation, or lost the following necessities: passion, care, purpose, success, fear, and revenge.

Remember them.

Passion

The burning love to do it! Ambition drives you to aspire to be a writer and compels you to take the action necessary to write your memoir. Strong passion intensifies ambition to finish your work, publish it, and launch it into the marketplace.

With my book *Sick as My Secrets*, I set a deadline for my fiftieth-class reunion. I drove myself to write my recovery story and step out of the shadows and be authentic after being thirty-five years sober. More importantly, this deadline coincided with a part of my life tied to the beginning of the memoir: my teenage years. My ambition intensified when I anticipated revealing this story.

Care

Value what you do. Contribute to the world and bring a caring energy to your work. Strive for a positive impact, and work from the heart through the soul in all you do. In other words, give a damn!

I absolutely love what I do with my writing life. I always focus on removing the stigma of a topic that negatively impacts women, such as I have done with domestic violence, alcoholism, and love addiction.

Purpose

Define your intention to the last degree. Live your dream with your words. Know where your compass lies and use it to guide you. Find your dreams by achieving your writing goals. Believe no reason to quit exists. Have faith in yourself and know what you are doing is on the mark.

I wrote my truth in my three memoirs and believed in what I was doing. I knew it was of value to other women who still suffered. I intend to continue to speak out on these important topics and serve as an advocate for change. I fiercely care about human issues; I don't shy away from them in my written words or when asked to speak. My books are meant to be of service. I allow myself to be guided by my faith as I write and rewrite every chapter. My desire is to create positives out of negatives.

Success

This reflects your desire to prosper. Are you ambitious enough to motivate yourself to good fortune? Your mindset to triumph over any odds may be reflected in your research or in your timeline to finish your desired project.

Working toward these goals will help:
- Maintain a strong yearning for success.
- Believe what you do is important to you and to others.
- Visualize yourself victorious despite the naysayers.
- Do whatever it takes to make it all happen.

By the time I set out to write my memoir on love addiction, I had experienced more than ten years of therapy and recovery in that area. I took time to step back, contemplate my situation, and learn more. By overcoming odds, my desire to succeed grew strong. I had a story to tell and knew I needed to get it out there, no matter what happened next. While difficult, I knew it was paramount to my success.

Fear

If you feel anxiety when you write, you must shake it off to move out of your comfort zone.

Consider these ideas:
- Perfect your craft. Empower yourself to overcome any fear or insecurity about entering the world of writing.
- Be willing to make personal sacrifices to finish your book.
- Find your peak performance hours to avoid writer's block.

- Allow the fear to go away and breathe deeply.
- Outrun your fear. Make the necessary changes to complete the job.
- Take no shortcuts while honing your skills.
- Put it all on the line, as if this is the last thing you will ever do.
- Be dedicated to challenging your work by engaging in a critique group.

My writing career is my last obsession. I waited a long time to do it. A lot of the fear that came with writing my memoirs, telling my truth, and advocating with my books has disappeared. I no longer fear retaliation from anyone I wrote about in my stories. I made sacrifices in time and money to publish my books just the way they happened. I saw no other way and discovered it had all been worth it. The feedback and connections they generated are priceless.

Revenge

Sometimes others may inflict harm to your reputation as an author. This can derail your writing career if you allow it.

Be ready to do the following:
- Mentally combat all the negativity coming your way.
- Grab hold of your ambition.
- Give yourself the gift of success and transfer it to your followers.
- Use a win from a writing contest to enhance your credibility.
- Don't settle for average. Redo that draft repeatedly.
- Join the elite group of writers who rise above criticism and negativity.
- Develop as a writer. Feel elated when you reach your goal.
- Don't waste energy on revenge.

- Accept the blessings that come and honor your internal success.
- Value your self-esteem and appreciate who you are as a writer.

I work at being a writer by journaling first and getting my thoughts on paper I pursue another book when it's time. Each book shows my progress. I value and appreciate myself as a writer. That is my wish for you. Just because I publish my books myself doesn't mean I shouldn't hold myself to a high standard, hone my skills, and value what I produce.

I leave you with these three types of ambition to help you analyze yourself on the state of your drive and determination, both to complete your book and to move on to the next one. They are *material ambition, production ambition,* and *creative ambition*. It's ambitious to stretch ourselves. It is crucial to ask if we're ready to succeed or even equipped for it.

Material ambition

This comes with a desire for awards and tons of sales. You fall short if you focus only on those items and ignore other professional details. You can be obsessed with gaining recognition to the point you spend so much time seeking notoriety that you lose sight of your purpose or your book's mission. We all desire material ambition, and we should. Yet we need to keep perspective and attend to our readers first and ourselves second.

Production ambition

Watch out for the temptation to cheat the reader by rushing to publication without taking the necessary steps to ensure a quality piece of work. Don't fail to conduct research to determine if a bookstore is right for your genre or book. Use a template to replicate the covers or characters from one book to the next. Being a prolific writer is ambitious and often impressive, but not at the expense of the reader. Even in this genre, which can include many books, you need to address various aspects of your life.

Creative ambition

I like to live here, in a writer's happy place to produce and find their voice.

Seek the following within yourself:
- Your drive to create.
- Your desire to write something new.
- Innovative ideas.
- Sophistication so the book can shine.

I often ask myself: Is my ambition too great? Am I cheating my readers? Am I rising to my abilities, or not? Can I publish more work? Am I courageous, or do I need to push myself more and be prouder of my work?

With all this in mind, I find peace and solace in writing. I allow my ambition to stay intact. This is who I am as a writer.

Activity: Narrative

1. Brainstorm your idea to draft a short essay or an important event with your writing partner or critique group.
2. Outline your essay as best you can from the feedback you received.
3. Practice writing it out in past tense.
4. Start writing with your attention-getter, your teaser, in mind.
5. Remember to include the where, when, and what.
6. Include what happened after.
7. Ask yourself how it changed you and how you felt before concluding this event.
8. Summarize your experience with this writing.

10. Journal to Write

The discipline of the writer is to learn to be still and listen to what her subject must tell her.

— Rachel Carson, American marine biologist

Journal writing is the practice of recording personal insights, reflections, and questions on assigned or personal topics.

Journal projects assigned in class may include your thoughts about daily experiences, reading assignments, or current events. These entries serve as a form of reflective writing. You can use them to consider or respond to something you have learned, read, or imagined yourself.

I've spent many years journaling. It is favorite habit of mine while I write memoirs and go through life learning about myself. I think things through instead of keeping them bottled up. Journaling has been a part of my writing life since I was a young girl and hid my diary beneath the mattress. I can safely talk to myself and get my feelings out on paper.

What to do

To learn to write a journal, give yourself time for the process. Each writer requires a different amount of time, be it minutes or hours. To succeed as a free-flowing writer, choose what comes to mind rather than a specific topic.

These ideas will help you start:
- Silence your phone before you begin.
- Write slowly rather than quickly to trigger your memory.
- Use your mind's eye to remember subjects, ideas, and scenes.
- Edit nothing and write more.
- Use your journal for personal commentary and problem solving.
- Doodle in your journal to sort out frustrations or make decisions.
- Carry your journal around during your day.
- Jot down the many things you've learned that day.
- Write about what you've resolved.
- Handwrite or type on your computer what you now question.

I kept a specific personal journal as a daily runner. By doing so, I developed my style and took on 10K races competitively here in Arizona for more than twelve years. While getting faster and faster, I tracked my personal time and miles. I visualized my success before every race by journaling. This journal writing supported my habit to run stronger.

My separate career journal focused on setting goals, meeting those goals, figuring out how to be more successful, and winning sales awards in the real estate business. I enhanced my professional life, especially when I started selling new homes. I wrote in my journal daily about everything that happened and evaluated what I could do better to be the top salesperson in the company. I enjoyed this highly competitive business, with my journal as my friend and partner.

How to do it

Writing daily or even a couple times a week may seem daunting to most writers. The idea is to give it a chance and make it work for you.

These tips will help you:
- Choose a more permanent bound journal.
- Keep it close and visible.
- Write in it at least once a day.
- Finish three to four pages each time you write.
- Use your favorite type of pen consistently.
- Try metaphors to describe your feelings.

Paramount to handling the many challenges that will come your way are your years of preparation. Sometimes your only option is your journal. Your journal pages take you back to the time when you wrote things clearly, from a new perspective.

Often, my emotions are all over my journal pages. At one time, my negative thoughts left a pattern I could not deny yet were valuable when writing my memoir on love addiction. Journal writing took me there and held the core of the story. Nobody else read it. If I thought for one minute someone had read these pages, I stifled my creativity and sabotaged the story. When I write a journal entry, I search for the words needed to describe something gnawing at me. This becomes my topic for the day.

Why do it?

You'll ask yourself these critical questions:
- What am I angry about?
- What disappoints me?
- Why do I feel this way?
- What part have I played?
- What brings me joy?
- What expectations do I have?

For whom do you write a journal?

The journaling process gives you the writing habits you will need to finish your memoir. Your stories will come easier because they're unfiltered. Your free writing moves you through your problems. You let them go on the page. You unclutter your mind and set yourself free from the stress and the chaos. Be open to the challenge and eager to begin, and this exercise will feel joyful and healing.

If you write in a notebook, you might discard the loose sheets. If you possess a bound journal, you keep these extraordinary gifts.

You've been shown how to do the following:
- Identify the significant part.
- Concentrate on showing, in detail, what is on your mind.
- Recollect, don't just document, your stories.
- Describe what your subconscious is feeling.

One of the saddest times in my life occurred the year after I was assaulted. I devoured a lot of therapy and worked in a dead-end job. Unable to move on after graduate school, I lived in a small apartment that was later damaged during a huge rainstorm. All my journals and many of my books, as well as a lot of my clothes, were spoiled beyond repair. My renter's insurance did not recover what was irreplaceable. None of it could be salvaged.

I felt tremendous despair losing my journals. They were my heart and soul, revealing to me what I observed in my life, what I expected, and how I felt about it all. In those pages, I put one thought ahead of another to open my mind and keep my stream of consciousness flowing. It took a while to regroup, but I did and continued to journal.

When is a suitable time?

Journal time is any time. A journal is for anyone who has that inner critic that says you can't do something. Many successful writers, such as Virginia Woolf, were prolific journal writers. She documented her writing progress in her journal and expressed how important her writing room was in her autobiography, *A Room of One's Own*.

I recommend the following questions as beginning prompts:

- What did I accomplish today?
- What are my goals for today?
- What would I like to accomplish this week? Next month? Next year?
- What ideas are on my mind?
- What things are gnawing at me?
- What am I most proud of today?

Today, I again boast piles of journals in my home office. I continue to be brutally honest on the page. My journaling habit is now second nature to me. Neither for the purposes of homework nor a deadline, the pages expose my soul to God only. I will use them later in my writing. I focus on what is in front of me to clear the clutter in my mind that day. I do not attempt to analyze problems necessarily but to seek answers or solutions naturally.

Seriously consider journaling in the morning—the earlier the better—when you are refreshed and ready to start the new day and clearly remember the revelations that came to you in the night. Attempt to unlock yourself from that unrelenting inner critic. This is your chance to clear out anything that lingers from the previous day, a chance to change your life with the swift movement of your pen.

Where can you journal?

Take your journal with you when you travel, locally or beyond. Pursue journal writing at every turn. While writing a memoir, keep it handy for unexpected inspiration or clarity. Ask yourself the tough questions. Be the interviewer, the investigator.

Here are a few more questions for your journal:
- What painful lesson did I learn this week?
- How can I avoid repeating my mistakes?
- What can I stop doing?
- What can I start doing?

When you're ready to start using your finished journals:
- Read your old entries with an open mind.
- Be sure you let them simmer for a few months or longer to get the best perspective on your stories.
- Do not get ahead of yourself.
- Read aloud and take each page seriously.

That page holds a valuable nugget for your memoir. Hopefully, you wrote slowly and distinctly the first time, and all the words mean something to you. As time goes on, remember you can easily imagine things that didn't happen, so read carefully and visualize what occurred in your mind's eye. This is your experience. Relive it fully. You conceive of and recollect the scenes in your own way to help create your stories.

Learn as you go

Your journals help you clarify your memory of events and what you want to write about. They are there to help you put your life in perspective and give you a clearer picture of what happened to you ten, twenty, or fifty years ago.
- Take time to study what you have written.
- Don't psychoanalyze yourself. Accept what you wrote and learn from it.
- Handwrite your journals, if you can, to grow closer to the subject.
- Bring your words to life in a journal, head, heart, and soul, by pen and paper.

My favorite journal is my gratitude journal. In it, I truly learn to know myself and prepare for memoir writing. Somedays, that is the only journal I engage in. It is the most important. I write a few pages and end with at least three things I am most grateful for at the time. They may be trivial things, such as having time to write, or huge things, such as my good health. Through this writing, I open up to a cheerful outlook about my life. I don't rant and rave about the difficult or wrong parts of it. There is truly little of that. I write on topics I need to address to make my existence better or open doors for my writing life.

Questions to prompt your gratitude journal writing:
- What three things am I grateful for today?
- What do I value most?
- Who helped me this week? This month?
- Who am I going to thank this week?

Once I am in this place of gratitude, the words begin to flow. I found the ideas and phrases I need and want to write that day. When I consistently journal, I discover ways to avoid writer's block. When I learn to think about my life and see myself for who I am, what I am made of, and what I can do, I write from my soul. This has been quite a learning experience for me. I highly recommend you do not miss the power of a gratitude journal.

Probe these questions in your gratitude journal:
- How should I have reacted in hindsight?
- How are things different now?
- What would I say to a younger version of myself?
- What lessons have I learned?

Teach yourself the art of journal writing

You can train your brain, through meditation or quiet concentration, to find ideas in your subconscious. You can develop those ideas in your journal and bring your stories to fruition. This supports your writing purpose. By writing three hundred words a day, or a page a day for ten days, you have your ten pages. Then you let it rest. Eventually, you redo draft one, two, and three. You get the idea.

This writing process produces 3,000 words for a chapter each month, or 6,000 words every couple of months, and eventually 72,000 words in a couple of years. This is a book. Of course, you can do more if life allows you to work faster. But, remember, a book needs to be nurtured. Don't rush your creativity. The average book today contains 80,000 words, something fully possible. When you journal with an open mind and heart, you are on your way to becoming an accomplished writer.

Consider several of the following, and make only one of them your own:

- A hardcover journal, standard size (8½ by 11) or a little smaller.
  - Feel how your handwriting embeds emotions into your subconscious.
  - Choose an attractive journal that calls to you.
- An app on your phone.
  - Accept the idea you are not physically connected with your soul.
  - See this as a more efficient choice.
- *The Artist's Way's* early morning pages program: www.juliacameronlive.com.
  - This foolproof method has worked for many people.
  - Understand this method takes time and discipline.
- One Note software, or another brand you prefer.
  - Realize you may not be free to write wherever you are.
  - Accept that it may feel more like work than joy.

Digest what is happening to you

Journal writing is not preplanned. You preplan your book goals. In your journal, you flesh out your stories and see your scenes more clearly. You become absorbed in your journal as you digest what happened to you and understand how the living you've done prepared you to tell your stories.

You may often experience a stream of consciousness in the moment because you have not cluttered your day with stressful items.

When this happens:
- Put your pen to the paper and do not edit.
- Write with fierce abandon.
- Promise yourself three pages.
- Find pure joy by writing in the fresh early morning.

By continuing to move forward, your mind takes you to innovative ideas, resolutions, and answers you have been searching for in your journal writing.

By not forcing your writing, a free flow of ideas can come forth from your subconscious. You have held these ideas for this exact time, as they have always been important to you. The words your subconscious found weeks ago are now ready to be put on paper. This can be anything personal to you. All parts of your life interconnect. By not editing these thoughts and storing them for another time, you internalize that connection, digest the material, and save the solution for your memoir pages.

Honor the master

Julia Cameron, the author of several books for writers, believes completing three journal-type pages each morning is paramount to your writing success. She contends this amount of writing, about 1,000 words, brings out your creativity and allows you to stay on topic later with your book. Three pages will be challenging at first. Shortly, three pages is what you will need to unlock your thoughts and start the juices flowing. Staying in the writing mode is critical to your success.

Allowing a stream of consciousness taught me to find what was stuck in my subconscious and bring it out. This was part of my therapy after being assaulted. I knew about this type of writing but had not truly practiced it until I joined a therapy group. Once I allowed my thoughts to spill out on paper, in the group, or with a therapist in an individual session, my mind freed up and I could spot the solutions. I learned to look for the solutions by trying not to filter any of what was coming through to me. I learned to process my anger in my journal and to forgive.

Value your journal

Make writing in your journal your main goal each morning, whichever journal or journals you choose to use. You're not showing this to anyone. These involve your genuine thoughts and darkest secrets, those you will contemplate for your memoir. Only some of these will come to life. Authenticity is the key. No appropriate agenda exists.

During the editing process of your memoir, your journal notes will help you:

- Describe in detail what you want to show us.
- Show us what you mean.
- Move to the important aspects of your writing.
- Recall the details of the incident.

To unblock your subconscious and see beyond the obstacles, avoid hiding the darkness. Go to the other side. You might choose to experience it again and make it your own. Even if you don't use all your journal writing and dumping, you will expel your fears and dark moods.

Perfectionism has always been a challenge for me. Never thinking I am good enough, that I need to keep doing things better. Writing in a journal is an imperfect form of writing for me since I do not spellcheck or edit. I leave my perfectionism out of the picture. To unblock myself, I allow myself to be messy, so it is all there. Then I decide what material is good for my memoir, considering what is relevant and what will be a good fit for the stories I am now ready to tell.

If you feel angry or have personal conflicts to work on, acknowledge and address them first, either with another person or in your journal. Then move forward. Try not to inhibit the flow of the journal. If you do, if you don't clean house, you stifle the authenticity of the memoir that follows. Any of the revelations you receive are gifts you can use to enrich your journal. Remember, in the beginning, you do not go back and read the journal. You fill your journal, then write your memoir pages and, lastly, go back to find the nuggets you left behind.

Keeping the habit

I keep a stone on my desk that a friend gave me a year ago. It reads, "Just Write." I look at it each time I sit down at my desk. No matter how I feel in the morning, I will feel better if I write something, anything, and especially if I write in my journal. If I do not keep up this habit, I will weaken my writing.

It is the same with my walking schedule, or my yoga classes, or my tennis days at the park. Consistency is the key. I do not allow myself to negotiate with my inner critic who talks me out of doing what is important to move my writing forward. Keeping this cheerful outlook about my writing, my book project, and my publishing goal impacts my entire day.

When you maintain a positive perspective, your subconscious can store things, events, and ideas differently, and you can retrieve them in the morning. If you believe you can learn while you sleep, you can journal and let it go in the evening, knowing your subconscious will have the solution the next day.

By getting into the habit of journaling, your other writing will follow suit. Making this a daily habit is like taking vitamins twice a day. It gives you a routine with a reward, a finished book. Prioritize your morning writing by setting time aside before you check emails or text messages. By choosing to write longhand, from mind to heart to soul to paper, and letting go of speed as the goal, you understand your thoughts and express your stories more clearly.

Activity: Journal starters

1. Brainstorm in your journal about a dozen keywords you enjoy.
2. Draft a story starter with at least three of them.
3. Consider writing an opinion or an argument.
4. Reflect on whether poetry or an exposition might work best for you.
5. Select a different route for a couple of your prompts.
6. Keep things open-ended.

11. Creativity

Making the simple complicated is commonplace, making the complicated simple, awesomely simple, that's creativity.

— Charles Mingus, American jazz pianist

You may often ask yourself: Is creativity a craft, a skill I can learn, an art I can share, or a God-given gift? There is more than one answer to understanding creativity and how to use it to your highest and best in writing.

Do you bring an analytical mind or an artistic mind to creativity? The truth is creativity stems from both. Creativity can be learned as a skill, through artistic expression with art or writing.

- You learn writing skills, stringing words together in sentence structure.
- You develop your prose by understanding English more fully as you write.
- You become more creative through your passion to produce stories in your own unique style.

There is no right or wrong way to do it. You can be an analytical type and do extensive research before you design a sentence, or you can be more artistic and free flowing by getting it all down on paper first, researching later.

Finding out which type you are, and how you will create, begins with what and how you read.

- If you read what you love, your writing will be more emotional and, thus, your readers will find your work more poignant.
- If you read for education only, underline and take notes with every page, and view everything you read as a lesson, your readers will feel you are teaching.

Both work with writing in the world of nonfiction. Anything goes. You educate, you motivate, you inspire, or you entertain, or all the above.

In each case, you do the following:
- Employ language skills to the fullest by building your vocabulary.
- Begin the manuscript and willingly advance your idea for the memoir.
- Develop your scenes.
- Seek creative, descriptive language to bring the reader into your story.

You want to weave compelling stories into the arc, or the lessons acquired in life. The goal is to take the reader to another place in time, or to a place they have never been, to catapult them to where you have been. With this philosophy, you captivate your readers' imagination, regardless of the theme of your book.

Becoming a creative channel

To become a creative channel, you must follow your inner guide, your intuition. Call it the higher power of the universe, or karma, or anything you like. There is much said about following your intuition with your creativity. You instinctively know exactly what you want to say, and you just keep writing and writing. Your artistic and creative energy leads you to produce your best work. These energies flow when you connect with your muse or another person. You know you are onto something, and you cannot stop.

When you are a creative channel for your art, your writing will touch your readers. This deep soul force is full and free consciousness. When you are there, in the zone, you will know it.

I experienced this when writing my first book. I was told it would happen if I had passion for the project. It did happen once I immersed myself in my writing. I was learning as much as I could about grief and dealing with grief for many years in the making. Eventually, I felt a surge of endorphins and kept going, writing faster and faster as I freed myself from any judgment.

Since that time more than twenty years ago, I have continued to experience this when I write. It occurs when I need to keep going, no matter the painful topic. I dig deep into my soul, a part of my creative channel, my inspiration from within.

This deep inspiration to perform is in all of us. You, too, can connect to your genius, your muse, in many ways:

- By using your skills, your talents, your passion, or a combination of all three.
- By being yourself.
- By allowing your channel to open for you.
- By trusting your intuition and acting on it.

Foster creativity

Writing memoir is creative writing, a form of creative nonfiction. To foster this form of writing, you offer thoughtful ideas, personal insights, intimacies about your life, and perspectives about the world you live in by doing the following:

- Work your innovative and emotional right brain.
- Use the analytical and mechanical left brain.
- See the analysis through your right brain too.
- Help the two sides work easily together with concentration on the task.
- Learn to write. It is a skill, and you can learn it to create your art.

- Enhance your creative genius with practice.
- Begin each day with writing and imaginative exercises.

You will produce more satisfying writing. Some of us are more creative than others, but we can all nurture the creativity we have been given and bring forth the inventiveness we have used in other areas.

Understanding new creativity

Think of new creativity as breaking out of your current mindset or a new way of thinking.
- Visualize a unique way of expressing yourself without losing your voice.
- Hear a new way of telling your stories that will engage your readers.
- Stay true to your vision in all this activity.
- Try not to go too far to your left or right brain in your thinking.

Your views on what you have learned from your experience could be skewed, causing undue stress. Trying to be too different is an indication you are not being authentic and may not display creativity in your writing. This is different than moving out of your comfort zone to grow with your writing. Being true to yourself is always the goal.

Keep in mind:
- Don't tear down what you know to be true about yourself.
- Don't eliminate the possibilities you've learned from your lessons. Your reader looks for those in your work.
- Step out of your "sandbox" for a good part of your manuscript.
- Examine what has worked in related stories you have written or in similar ideas you have proposed from your experiences.

- Capitalize on those solutions by allowing yourself to draft a compelling story with an enticing teaser at the end of each chapter.
- Lean into how you have changed and how your life has improved or grown from your experiences.

Remember the words of Pablo Picasso: "I am always doing that which I cannot do, in order that I may learn how to do it."

Learn to understand, experience, and communicate the current knowledge you hold about your story—what happened to you and to the others in your stories—before you walk out of that scene into the next. By listening to your intuition, the solution may appear right under your nose. Following your intuition is always well advised.

- Take time to look at another's thinking in their "sandbox" of writings and ask yourself what you find good about it.
- Read other memoirs or creative nonfiction work in your theme and topic areas.
- Know what is out there, who your competition is.
- Get feedback from your critique group, writing in the same genre.
- Join a general writers' group and connect with a writing partner or editor for help as you develop your manuscript.
- Put yourself in the shoes of others while on the path of creativity and writing.

No limits

You will have no limits if you are open to surpassing other writers.

Hear the words of Joseph Clinton Pierce: "To live a creative life, we must lose our fear of being wrong."

The author of more than twelve books on human development and spirituality, he leads from a place of positivity on writing. I appreciate his attitude and hope you do too.

He suggested the following:
- Give creativity a chance to rise.
- Encourage yourself and your writing tribe, your critique group, and writing group, regardless of risks.
- Tell your truth, be open, share all, go deep.
- Give yourself and your group space to explore projects from the right and left sides of the brain.
- Allow members and yourself time to transform.
- Set goals and deadlines and reward yourself with "free thinking" time every day.

Consider descriptive and realistic monthly goals as you move forward and develop more of your writing plan.

I recommend the following:
- Look in your "sandbox" often and determine whether the walls have crumbled a bit due to your creative expression.
- Visit others in your tribe to learn from them.
- Look at solutions or research options you have never considered that might take you deeper into your topic or theme.
- Structure your ideas a bit differently than first thought, even ones you passed on or did not use in a previous book or article.

Boost your creativity to write

Maya Lin, artist and architect, said, "Sometimes I think creativity is magic; it's not a matter of finding an idea but allowing an idea to find you!"

Creativity does not have to be found or shown to you. Be ready for it. It just comes to you when you are ready, willing, and open. When, instead of insisting you follow your mind map or outline, put it down, lose yourself in your simple side of life, and let ideas find you. You discover your uniqueness by leaving your desk or office behind to take a walk or a leisurely rest in nature.

Write the Memoir You're Afraid to Write

While inviting innovation to come with you, you seek inspiration and transformation, not force it to happen.

I have been asked many times, "How do you get your ideas? How do you create your stories beyond just your memory?"

My answers are:
- Walk away from the stories, many of which are initially difficult to put on paper.
- Allow your ideas to be nurtured in your soul.
- Give your ideas time to germinate and grow in your heart so they are ready to be part of your work.

At least every six months, I reorganize my desk and office and throw a couple garbage bags of trash away. I start with the collection of items I've retained from expos and workshops I've attended. I purge a lot. I recycle used paper for writing drafts.

I recently replaced all the hanging folders in both my desks and my credenza with brightly colored hanging folders—five assorted colors to liven up my office and spur my creative thoughts. I found this menial task energizing. It gave the drawers a fresh look when opened. Doing this gave me time to focus on a part of my current chapter that had stalled. It resulted in a crisp approach to my writing.

By doing these mindless tasks, I can:
- Release stress.
- Forget things and enjoy the manual labor.
- Stand, squat, or sit on the floor and embrace the change from sitting in front of the laptop.

When I return to the screen, I am rejuvenated and ready to go. Later in the day, after purging, sorting, and trashing, I go down to the Jacuzzi in the neighborhood. Since I do not want to be disturbed, I choose an area I think will be less busy.

This is great "think time" for me. I discover how I should do something differently or structure something on which I am working. Evening is best because I am most productive in the morning. I do this activity later in the day when I need to release stress. To understand more, see the activity at the end of this chapter.

Ideas to boost your creativity:

- Listen to music that relaxes or inspires.
- Brainstorm with someone you trust.
- Bring a notebook wherever you go.
- Increase your vocabulary.
- Define your problem in detail.
- Exercise and take quiet time.
- Watch inspirational programming.
- Be mindful of mood-altering substances.
- Read everything you can.
- Exercise your brain like your body.

The last and most prominent place to allow your ingenuity to flow is in your writing space. A creative office is an imaginative place. It will promote innovation just by its existence.

My office is painted khaki green with light maple wood floors and new windows framed in cream with no window coverings. We live on the seventh floor, so do not require window coverings. The sunlight invites me into the room. I do not feel as if I'm stuck in a cave. The windows are tinted so the sun is never too harsh. We removed all our shutters and blinds last year to create a spacious and positive environment.

This space features a desk and credenza with a matching filing cabinet in cherry wood. A second, older, more traditional Ethan Allen desk and a bookshelf, also in cherry wood, provide storage. I display inspirational works of art and personal pictures on the wall, including my book covers and my husband's too. Other stimuli near my desk include my "Just Write" rock and my green alabaster four-leaf clover paper weight. I work to keep my office unburdened of clutter.

I also write at the local library. I am incredibly careful when I do so as not to restrain my creativity. The local library offers writing spaces. I prefer to use them only in the off-hours when extra activity, like story hour for the little ones, isn't scheduled.

If I write in a coffee shop, I go to the larger cafés. I go in the afternoon hours and find a writing space in a corner for a quieter experience. In Scottsdale, we can write outside for many months of the year. I don't write out-of-doors with my laptop. When I've printed my work after a first or second rendition, editing it by hand, outside and away from a crowd, gets my creativity going in another direction.

Many times, just being in the early morning fresh air spurs on better editing. But wherever I write or create, words come, and pages are written. I am receptive to my intuition and have faith it will always be there.

Activity: Finding your creativity, your muse.

1. The simplicity of mindless endeavors is a powerful muse. They are free and available to any writer at almost any time. Write on the following. Select one and "just do it."
2. What mundane task can you do tonight to release stress and generate creativity?
3. Where will you go tomorrow to take a break from your writing?
4. What will you do during your "think time" interlude to refresh your mind?
5. What is your favorite thing to do to slow down and create more proficient writing?

12. Success

The difference between a successful person and a failure often lies in the fact that the successful man (woman) will profit by his (her) mistakes and try again in a unique way.

— Dale Carnegie, American writer and lecturer

Norman Vincent Peale once said, "Throw your heart over the fence and the body will follow."

If you fear success, this quote may apply. Writing a memoir can create a lot of fear and apprehension. It is human nature to feel trepidation at various times in your writing life. We all feel it, especially if we take on something new. Writing your first memoir, or even your second if you're going to be more transparent, can generate much uneasiness. As you succeed, more people will read your books, and you will have much notoriety. You have more to risk but also gains to enjoy.

You give fear power when you resist facing it. It's better to just go with it. By acknowledging this possibility, you become less fearful of success and more energized to start, continue, and finish your memoir. Your mantra could be, "I accept my fear of success," while moving on to draft your stories. Eventually, you will know some form of success is dependent on you overcoming your fears.

Here are ways to positively address your uneasiness:
- Learn how to speak to promote your book by going to Toastmasters, for instance.
- Allow estrangement from someone at the risk of authenticity.

- Ignore jealousy from others when you do succeed.
- Avoid naysayers if your robust success is questioned.

Only when you fear writing your memoir do you stretch yourself. You risk scrutiny to help others and add value to your readers. This can be a fulfilling experience for you as a writer. You grow as a storyteller by not avoiding your fear. With success, and by being transparent and forthcoming with your stories and ideas, life can be unsettling.

Accept the following:
- Be strong in mind, body, and spirit.
- Prepare for success, however it comes.
- Understand that success breeds success.
- Live your success repeatedly.

Contemplate this phenomenon of visualizing success. Give these concepts some thought as you write your manuscript:
- Stay focused on your well-defined goals, regardless of other people's perceptions.
- Keep growing your writing skills and honing your craft to see just how far you can go as a recognized writer.
- Prepare to be asked for advice as an expert in your genre once you publish. Take pride in this position.
- Understand jealousy can arise in anything, so don't be afraid to justify your convictions and your writing and defend yourself.

Amazon's success and you

If you read books, buy books, or draft books, you have heard of and dealt with Amazon. Amazon is the most incredible outlet ever invented for all authors and every genre of books. It was named after the Amazon River, the largest river in the world. Amazon is now celebrating more than thirty years in business. However you feel about its incredible success—good, bad, or

Write the Memoir You're Afraid to Write

indifferent—it has dominated your life as a reader and book buyer for a long time. It will impact the rest of your writing days as an author.

To go forward, you should know:
- Amazon sells fifty percent of all print books and seventy percent of all e-books.
- Nobody really knows how many books are on Amazon.com, though estimates tout at least ten million books listed for sale.
- Nobody really knows how many books sell each year on Amazon.com, but they sell more books than anyone else.
- The company's market share continues to grow every year.

As an author seeking success, you must at least consider listing your title on Amazon.com. You have almost no choice in the matter. Amazon's existence, if you join them, will help deliver your success in everything you do publishing and marketing your books. For your journey to success, please come to grips with this idea now. Life will be easier for you. Regardless of how you feel about any of the above information, it is your new reality.

As they say in some circles, "You must go with the flow of the Amazon River," and not fight it upstream. Use the power of Amazon to work to your advantage. You can immediately try many possibilities that have worked for many authors.

Here are only a few to consider before finishing your manuscript:
- Write an impressive and succinct description for your Amazon author page.
- Make it exceptional to compete with the extensive number of books on its site.
- Have the verbiage edited by a professional and made as enticing as possible.
- Read other descriptions for ideas.

- Visualize your success when you think of Amazon.
- Know Amazon wants you to succeed, sell books, and make money.

You can't beat them, so join them. Peruse the free Author Central account page provided for you, along with the following:

- Create your author bio immediately.
- Have a professional photo done and ready.
- Once in place, manage your book and book reviews.
- Update the way your book is displayed on the page often.

Begin to focus your energy on how to target potential readers. Amazon never shares who buys your book or others' books, or who has read anyone's books. You can see what else your readers bought once they've purchased yours. You can begin to identify the type of person buying from you by what else they buy. Go to your book detail page and review the section entitled *"Customers who bought this item also bought..."*

If some fans liked your book and your competitor's book, why wouldn't all fans like your book? Consider buying advertising targeting your ideal reader. Remember, sales ranking references sales on Amazon. It reports recent sales of your book on an hourly basis.

To find your book's ranking, do the following:

- Go to product details for your book.
- Don't obsess about your ranking.
- Value your book for what it means to you.
- Understand your rank is tied to the success of your marketing activity.
- Track the catalyst driving these changes.

After analyzing your situation, consider what motivated readers to buy. By determining your marketing activities, you can motivate readers to buy in the future. Where possible, duplicate any actions you saw that worked for other Amazon books, and continue to peruse Amazon to see what is happening.

When you keep track of what has worked in the past, you visualize your memoir's success on the biggest stage.

Do the right things to make this happen:
- Study successful authors on Amazon.
- Be sure you have a book cover that stands out, especially in thumbnail size.
- Ask people to buy your book, read it, and review it.
- Request readers draft book reviews for you.
- Ask them to tell their friends on social media.
- Offer free copies to Amazon's top reviewers.
- Run book giveaways.

Remember, Amazon is not a cult, but it is very secretive. You can only guess how many books are on their website, how many are selling, and how many are added every day. Relish the competition. Imagine the possible rewards you could achieve with this phenomenally successful vehicle if you use all the tools offered to you. Be willing to maneuver your way through Amazon. Success can be yours if you become a savvy marketer and enjoy your ride on the River Amazon.

Your success

To be a successful writer of memoir, you must also consider doing some or all the following, in your own way, and at your own pace:
- Believe writer's block does not exist.
- Write with the goal of being read.
- Develop a distinctive writer's voice for yourself.
- Understand what makes you who you are as a writer of memoirs.

To appreciate your success as a writer, recognize the following:
- A little raw talent.
- Originality through your eyes.
- A true love for reading.

- Craftsmanship as learned artistry.
- The art absorbed in your soul.
- Imagination and daydreaming, curiosity.
- A compelling reason to challenge yourself.
- Hard work and cathartic success.

By seeing all sides of your ideas, and others' perspectives on your stories, success will come from being open-minded and keeping your ears and eyes ready for the new and different, even though you're telling your truth.

When you are fully aware things are not black and white, especially with memoir, you are able to investigate and do your research. You will experience more awakenings as you pursue this approach. You will make the most of your story by not just running on emotion, but by setting up a structure and a plan for what you are willing to do. When you are set up for success, you will find a deeper calling and a compelling story after the first or second draft. You will no longer fear the thought, *Will I receive a lot of heat?* and carry on.

This is your golden time for writing success, or you would not be making the time to do it. By going big with your ideas and plans, you let go of the ideas and accept the success or rejection that comes. Always keep in mind the original intent of your theme, the core story. Be willing to create relationships through your information, help others, and inform and educate your readers.

Recap of writing success:

Choose the following for your success as a writer and future author:
- Identify yourself as the writer on your business card.
- Submit your work to a critique group, writing mentor, or coach.
- Practice perseverance. Show up and do the work every day, no excuses.

- Master more than one skill after storytelling, speaking, goal setting, or marketing.
- Be kind and generous with other writers in your groups.
- Be consistent with your storytelling in all ways.

Congratulations on your greatness, your dedication, and your determination. Just write.

Looking back thirty plus years, I am sure the company I worked for was concerned about being sued for harassment or discrimination. Management knew they had to do the right thing, so they hired a woman. Me. The pressure was on. I was in the right place at the right time, and I took advantage of it all. My commitment to writing specific and manageable goals and reaching them was exciting yet stressful in many ways. I worked late into the evenings and on weekends for more than twenty years. I learned much about people's needs, the benefits they need to decide to buy, and how goals, desire, perseverance, and persistence can pay off.

Activity: Setting goals for writing success

- Write incremental goals for your memoir daily, weekly, and monthly.
- Write these goals in a bound notebook or on your computer.
- Visualize your success at every turn using this SMART approach:
    - *Specific*: Clarify what, how, and when you will write. Determine exactly what your topic, theme, or chapter goal will be for that day, week, or month.
    - *Measurable*: Make your goals tangible so you and others can see them. Set number goals and match them to your desires.
    - *Achievable*: Be realistic with the size of the goal for each week. Make the goal fit the

- *Relevant*: Stay on task with your writing project in relationship to your goals. Consider which goals are more relevant and important for you now rather than later.
- *Time-limited*: Set an endpoint and make it happen. For example, decide when pages are due to your critique group each month and meet that endpoint. Set small goals for the day or the week, keeping the main goal and the big picture in mind.

A few more tips:

- Set goals you control and visualize your success.
- State your goals in positive terms and feel them happening.
- Prioritize your goals for your writing project.
- Work backward from the main goal to monthly, weekly, and daily.
- Share your goals with writer friends you trust.
- Revisit your goals often to make them your own.

13. Break the Rules

The young man knows the rules,
but the old man knows the exceptions.

— Oliver Wendell Holmes,
former associate justice of the Supreme Court

Creative people break the rules of writing, as described in many books and articles. You especially see this in memoirs and nonfiction, often embedded in the format and structure of storytelling. You might also see rules broken with dialogue. The nonfiction genre is usually a free space and an opportunity for the author to be authentic, to rebel, and to see it through their own eyes.

Initially, you may judge a broken rule, thinking it disregards the readers' expectations, refuses to conform, and disobeys what you have always known. You may consider the author irresponsible when they ignore what needs to be done to give the story a good flow. It is quite the opposite for creative types, especially memoir writers. When creating your own stories, you write in a format conducive to storytelling, to be intriguing and display behavior that entices, not necessarily consents to the norm. You must express yourself within your own style and voice.

Your main goal as a memoirist is to bring the reader into your life, into your deepest emotions and experiences, as well as into your heart and soul. By complying with the rules, you might appear to be treating your readers gently, when that does not reflect your story. To tell your true story, you cannot go along in harmony. You must not be afraid.

The rule breaker

If you're a writer who breaks the rules, like I am, this is your time and place to write your memoir. Enjoy! More memoirs are published in unusual formats than ever before. Some cross over to nonfiction self-help or how-to books, like mine. I crossed over my last two memoirs by doing much research on the main themes. Even as an authority with experience in love addiction, domestic violence, recovery, post-traumatic stress, and grief, I went further with in-depth research.

As a memoir writer, you'll be tempted to break the rules often to create what you want, just as an artist who breaks out in modern art. The key is to know when not to go too far, injure your work, harm your dream, or stifle your goals. You don't need to be the martyr to be effective. You can still share your important struggles. You're not the suffering victim anymore. You're the strong voice of experience.

To be aware of this approach, consider the following:

- If you break a writing rule, such as in dialogue, make it noteworthy.
- If you break a format rule, such as adding a special chapter, think it through.
- If you break a structure rule, such as moving the peak moment of the story, justify your decision to the reader with a fact or two.
- If you break a rule repeatedly, be proud of your choices.

Rules are meant to be broken

Some believe the rules of writing are meant to be broken, while others are afraid to break these rules. You choose who you are as a memoir writer.

- Are you afraid to write the memoir you were meant to write, or are you afraid to write in general?
- Are you a literary rule breaker?

- Are you one who needs permission to author your story?
- Are you one who would not tell your inner most secrets?
- Are you a conformist or a rebel?
- Are you writing the tantalizing memoir or the one that leaves us on the outside?

At times, breaking rules does limit you more than it enables you. Be sure you are on the right path to understanding your stories. Retell them several times to yourself and a confidant. Wrest them from your soul before you write them.

Use proper jargon, words distinctive to the locale in which the story exists, or you may weaken your story and lose readers. At the same time, you don't want to make them feel like outsiders. Replace clichés with fresh, innovative wording to capture all your audiences. Show us, don't tell us, with the use of detailed descriptions.

Other important questions are:
- Can you start a fire underneath your writing?
- Do you lead with writing?
- Can you be an advocate for a cause?
- Do you know the purpose of your memoir?

Inventive minds know

People with the most creative mindsets are more likely to break the rules because they are naturally living outside the norm. The more creative writers become, the easier it is for them to tell their story in a way that justifies writing without limitations.

They will:
- Break the rules and spark a fire for attention.
- Evaluate the consequences for success.
- Stick to their values while doing their best work.
- Maintain proficient writing.

- Check for wordiness, grammar, and flow.
- Develop the characters, the plot, and the theme.

I strongly encourage you to consider ways to feel free to break a few writing rules and express yourself more deeply. Risk exploring what you don't know versus voicing what you do know, a choice key to writing a memoir.

Write what you don't know

In an earlier chapter, I mentioned the common theme of "write what you know," which I believe is often overused in memoirs. While drafting three memoirs, I wrote about things I didn't know. I expanded my thoughts through research, observation, and interviews.

You write your truth based on your beliefs, then enhance your stories with facts and information that teach you more and open your mind.

Solutions:
- Use facts that are understandable and relatable to your audience.
- Know what fits your readers by doing extensive research on who is reading your type of book or similar books in your genre.
- Spend time doing a competitive analysis of who is reading what kind of book.
- Ramp up your solutions and ideas to solve your book's issues.

As you write a memoir and bring up your memories, you learn more about yourself and carry that information forward. With this added knowledge, you can expand on what you don't know and enhance the story for yourself and your readers. By encouraging your audiences to exercise some faith as they read your stories, they search for their own solutions and resolutions. These stem from their own knowledge and interest in the subject.

I experienced this when I wrote my second memoir, *Three Husbands and a Thousand Boyfriends*. I had lived with love addiction for decades and had no idea how that impacted me. For a long time, I did not know what was wrong with me or understand what I had experienced. I went through an outpatient treatment program while in the throes of love addiction. My treatment focused on anger management, childhood abandonment, and fear-related loneliness. My shortcomings challenged me, particularly fear and anger. They stood out.

No one mentioned love addiction directly but suggested I read a couple of books. One addressed the topic head-on. I recognized myself at once after reading a few chapters. I wanted to learn more. By reading Pia Mellody's *Facing Love Addiction*, I felt compelled to research others online. I attended workshops and studied everything I found on the topic. I became an authority and strengthened my message.

By the time I wrote my memoir on love addiction a few years later, I gained a good perspective on the subject. I took the time to come full circle and heal. I prided myself on acknowledging my problem. Because of this realization, I wrote my memoir as an authority and pledged to do decent work.

Discipline yourself

Discipline is a dirty word to some of you, especially those with free-thinking, inventive minds. You cringe at self-discipline when it means setting a schedule, writing so many hours a day, or producing so many words a month. As writers, we all struggle with discipline. The "breaking the rules" notion is much easier to grasp. Still, they go together. When you understand both, you can still have fun.

As a writer, you follow your dreams and look to reach the lofty goal of authoring a book or producing an article or screenplay, usually with a deadline. This is still a joyous way to go. Despite the rewrites and the editing process, you take pride in all you do. Using discipline to set up a structure for your work gives you permission to break a few rules elsewhere.

The process, practice, and pride of writing does not allow for wasted time. In my own way, it's discipline, not obsession. My writing is a divine gift, bringing my heart and soul to the experience. By initially holding my pen, through my work, I cast my words on the page that later reached my laptop. My goal with writing memoir focuses on stripping it down Hemingway style, using the fewest words to make my point. Search for the real story quickly but sufficiently, and work to make every word important.

It is often easy to write, and write, and overly write when in your zone. You need to be disciplined, even if you break the rules and use a longer sentence when a shorter one is good or truer to your voice.

A conference speaker once said, "To improve your writing, cross out every other word."

I almost cried. My attachment to my writing was too great to even think of such a thing. Of course, it was said in jest but helped us consider how verbose our work can be.

As a writer, you are given many rules for discipline. Some are cliché to me today. Although I have heard them many times, they are still valid and worth noting.

Break Rule #1: It's a journey, not a race.

The calendar is important and deadlines matter, but a book takes as long as is needed. There is a different timeline for all books and all writers. You must take the time you need to do your best. Do not rush to publication and risk making mistakes you will later regret. Take the book's cover design, for example. It must grab attention, entice readers to pick it off shelves easily, or click online even more quickly. Spend the time you need to get it right.

Break Rule #2: Strap yourself in your chair and write.

This rule sounds like good advice, but it is not fair to you if you break the discipline rule. This guilt-ridden comment has no place in the busy lives of writers, especially those with other obligations. Writing for a few hours at a time works for me; then I need to take a break. I read, research, walk, or attend an appointment. I do not push myself to exhaustion and become unavailable when a new idea comes forth from my subconscious.

Break Rule #3: Don't whine and just do it.

You can't complain. Writing is a privilege. Most of us have had other careers before our writing life and know what it takes to support decorum. We have this discipline thing figured out and can bring it back when we need it. We might voice our dislike for something, breaking the rules a bit. Still, we know what needs to be done. For more than twenty years, I've carried out most of my goals by fitting my writing into my bursting schedule.

Break Rule #4: Writing is twenty percent inspiration.

Don't read your reviews. Inspiration motivates. With all my books, I was driven to be a vehicle for the voiceless, an agent for change, and a willing spokesperson who stood up and spoke out. You may be in the same or similar place with your memoir, or you may be inspired by someone else's memoir to draft your story and eventually motivate others. May the person you dedicate your book to be the one who inspired you. Whatever your situation, useful content and even better writing and editing will take you far, but that twenty percent of inspiration will keep you afloat.

Writing spaces

You can "break the rules" with your writing spaces. Whether you use a laptop or write first in longhand, you can do it your way. You might write in the park, in your home office, in the library, or at the dining room table.

If I write in a coffee shop, I tune out the noise with earplugs or sheer determination. Whatever your thing is, you do not need adopt the role of the traditional writer hunkering down at home in a quiet space alone for hours, unless that works for you.

At various times, all the above work for me. If I am writing new material, I might draw pictures that arise from my heart, my soul, and my subconscious. I go to that free space where breaking the rules happens. I might also talk to myself and work off my storyboard or mind map. These different approaches allow freedom of expression, one with pictures and the latter with words and drawings. Brainstorming with another author—

reviewing revisions I've made from feedback from a critique group or writing partner—serve me as well.

My critique group members limit our submissions each month to about a dozen pages to help with time constraints. That said, I make every effort to stay close to twelve pages, knowing my chapter will be stronger in the end given the average reader today reads less. After taking a second and third look for excessive adjectives and meaningless verbiage, I continue to shoot for no fluff. The practice of brevity is not easy for any writer, and certainly not for this writer. My goal is always to go to that place of powerful writing that shows my intention and speaks the language of the human experience.

In summation

Write, revise, and finish your project within a realistic deadline. Make it a great piece of work, then revise it one more time. Set a goal of disciplining yourself to be a concise writer.

Practice choosing a writing project with basic human emotions:

- The joy of another person in your life.
- The sadness of being lonely in a crowded world.
- The experience of getting closer to God.
- The grief of losing another person dear to you.

Remember to congratulate yourself along the way, and certainly when you've finished. Most people do not have the perseverance to pursue a writing career or to set a goal to finish a memoir. Be proud of yourself. You are following your dream and will change lives. You will make connections and engage people with something they've been looking for in their writing. Along the way, you will have broken a few rules to set you free.

Before believing you have a finished product, remember to do the following:

Use strong verbs.

Verbs perform a job. Make them good and specific to a task. Be direct with them and make sure they are powerful. On your next revision, highlight your verbs, and ramp them up a notch. Don't depend solely on a thesaurus. Be precise.

Avoid passive voice.

Use simple past or present tense. In most cases, avoid a using a "to be" verb—was, have, am, being—before an -ed or -ing word: "She was planning/is planning to be a writer" uses passive voice "She planned/plans to be a writer" is active voice. It is okay on occasion to break this rule.

Limit adverbs.

Cut words such as "then," "just," "of course," "etcetera," and most "-ly" words that modify a verb. Rarely use "really" or "very."

Show, don't tell.

Give us all the juicy details in the action, rather than simply stating it does occur. Let the reader experience the story through the "character's" five senses instead of distancing them from the action by using narrative.

Write authentic dialogue.

Don't try to impress. Rules can be broken here. Avoid too much slang or vernacular. Ask yourself how those in your story would naturally speak. Remember how you speak. Read dialogue aloud to hear how natural it sounds.

If you have a tough time writing succinctly, try reading Hemingway. He was an incredible writer. When it came to making a point and tightening up writing, he was the expert. Make yours a great piece of work. Then revise it one more time. Set a goal of disciplining yourself to be a concise writer.

Activity: A "free" writing project

Choose one of these basic human emotions:
1. The joy of another person in your life.
2. The sadness of being lonely in a crowded world.
3. The experience of growing closer to God.
4. The grief of losing another person close to you.

Review this chapter before you start writing about the emotion and think of all the ways you can "break the rules" and make the project your own. Keep the writing to about 350 words, then try to revise it to 250 words.

14. Audience

The one who listens is the one who understands.
— African proverb

Focusing on your intended audience from the very beginning of your writing is critical. This group of readers listens to you and reads your work. Crucial to your success, they are paramount to the value of your memoir. Write to that audience.

Your target audience is narrower than your potential market. They matter tremendously to reaching your goals. Your goal is to touch them deeply with your words and stories. If you do, they will show interest in your book immediately. Understanding who your ideal readers are as a demographic group will help you reach them. You accomplish this by researching online and in bookstores and talking to other authors. You can begin focusing on this topic before or during the writing of your memoir.

Keep this concept in your consciousness as you move forward with your writing. Dig deeper to develop and refine your stories for them. Your compassion and motivation will shine through.

Your target readers will do at least one of four things:
- Be receptive to your message.
- Be apathetic about what you present.
- Be uninformed about your topic and need educating.
- Be hostile about your topic, requiring respect for their viewpoints.

Use the following recap questions to help narrow your audience and write your memoir keeping your readers:

What is your memoir about?

You must be able to tell the reader this in less than thirty seconds. If you can't do that now, work on it until you can do it quickly. Read or give your answer to a trusted critic. Convey this information openly to anyone who asks. Grasp the importance of this exercise.

I carry bookmarks in my purse and am ready with my thirty-second blurb. I can describe on cue what my books are about and what benefits the person who reads them will gain. I've worked on this two-prong approach repeatedly and enjoy the interaction with potential readers.

What types of people are interested in your theme?

Give this question much thought. Brainstorm your answer with your writing partner, your critique group, or other writing friends. Consider race, gender, culture, education, career, hobbies, and marital status. Observe who buys your competition's books on Amazon or in bookstores.

I continuously think about who my next reader might be and how to find them. I don't dismiss any reader possibility and review all that may apply.

What organizations might be interested in your theme?

- Evaluate your purpose to find these organizations where your readers spend time together.
- Understand the message you want to communicate to them.
- Visualize them benefiting from reading your book.
- Put yourself in your reader's shoes.

By seeing the big picture, I was able to open the doors of support from various organizations. I became conscious of what was available to me which helped it happen. My partnerships with national organizations came along by being visible on social media.

Is your audience female, male, or both?

Writing to a male-dominated audience is far different than writing to a women's market. Many reasons are apparent. Race and culture make it more complicated. Understanding how these audiences cross over can impact the success of your book. Often a book is intended for one of these audiences and is also appealing to both. Be ready for this to happen. Books on health and wellness have proven this point, as men are now much more interested in their health.

My audiences are primarily female, but my memoir on domestic violence sells to men as well as it does with women. I stay on top of these types of trends.

Is most of your audience under or over forty?

This is the demarcation line for many memoirs. When a book is written for the over-forty crowd, it is well received by both baby boomers and their children. The younger generation, those closer to forty, may read it to understand their parents or grandparents. They may also have an infatuation with the era.

I do talks at treatment centers and recovery homes for attendees twenty to sixty years old, male and female, gay and straight. These issues are universal, and the audience members are open to discussion, which works well for memoirs. In the more than two years of doing this, I've only had one disruptive male who was immediately removed from the room.

Are most of your audience members college educated?

Write to this level of reader and assume they are with you. Most newspapers in the United States are written to an eighth-grade reading level, the average reading level in our country. *The*

Wall Street Journal is written at an eleventh-grade reading level. That said, by using too many "hoity toity" words, you display arrogance and can lose your audience.

I write for understanding and in the way I speak and communicate in conversation. When in doubt, I keep it simple. It's the same way I learned to author articles for national company newsletters.

How much do your readers already know about your subject?

- Do not assume your audience is as informed as you are on your topics.
- Do not be condescending in your approach.
- Always consider they are reading your book to learn.
- Give helpful information to entice the reader to seek more knowledge.

Each of my last two memoirs offers appendices in the back of the book with resource lists and other suggestions. When I share from the depths of my soul, I take the reader from despair to hope with information on where to find help or help somebody else. You never know who might need a phone number, an online resource, or further reading options. I give them plenty of information to go forward and pursue the desired results. The mission is always to help others.

What do your readers need to fully comprehend your memoir?

Give the background on why you are writing the memoir, what it means to you, who influenced you, and what your purpose is. Share this in your introduction. Give them your soul-stirring moments, your authentic self, your truth, the lessons you have learned, and the path to transformation. They seek this. They want to learn and grow from your experience and resolve.

Nowhere in my writing do I condemn anything I've done. I treat myself with grace and dignity while telling my story. I give myself forgiveness. I write on topics that could cause guilt and shame, but I do not accept those emotions. This frees the reader too.

How will your readers gain the most from your memoir?

- Give them sincere and honest dialogue.
- Write these conversations to the best of your ability.
- Bring them into the scenes of your story with intriguing talk.
- Allow them to feel a part of your experience.
- Help them relate their situations to yours.
- Show them your dark side, that part you share with only a few.

I don't hold back in my stories. I write the memoir I was afraid to write. I invite readers deep into my soul. The good and the not-so-good are all out there. Helping others is a gift of a professionally written memoir.

What do most of your readers have in common?

Your readers have a lot in common with you. They buy the same types of books you do and seek out the same movies. They even appreciate the art and other cultural offerings you enjoy. These similarities are valuable to the memoir writer. We feel freer to tell our stories, knowing our readers want to learn more about how we overcame the obstacles and challenges of our life. They'll honor the genre with the purchase of your book.

The best part of a speaking event is meeting and talking to the people who eventually buy my book. I love to find out how much we have in common. I can tell in the first few minutes of greeting them how many are potential readers of my work. I sense my soulmates. They nourish me during any workshop.

Do most of your readers engage in the same hobbies? What are they?

Assume your audience is a lot like you. They will be interested in health and wellness if you are, or in acceptance and forgiveness if those are an important part of your work. If you focus on death-defying sports, you will attract readers who do too. It usually works out that way.

I've often observed this when signing books, or reading my emails or Amazon reviews. I've enjoyed this part of my ride.

Do most of your readers follow similar career paths? What are they?

If my theory continues to work, their careers will be freer spirited if you are. Or more disciplined if that is your nature. Then again, you could have a fringe audience looking to see how the other half lives, who enjoys your work despite their different nature. Things happen in life to people of all races, genders, classes, and socioeconomic statuses. Many times, our readers live vicariously through our lives and read our stories regardless of who they are or where they've been.

I have enjoyed this experience with my book on recovery from alcohol. Women are drinking more, especially younger women. The interest in women and alcohol has grown. I benefitted from good timing for my book. It is beginning to show in the feedback I receive.

When you conceived of the idea for your memoir, who did you imagine reading it?

Imagine your friends and family first because they know you, love you, or at least care about you. The bigger picture embraces the world of people out there seeking to read memoirs by authors they don't know. They appreciate your memoir, you, and your work, unequivocally.

Many times, the memoir writer feels highly disappointed that friends and family do not read their work. Work with this reality as you write.

My husband received a terrific response to his first memoir, although not from his immediate family. His friends have enjoyed it immensely, along with others from book events or online sales. The best surprise? His grandson did a book report on his memoir for school and earned an A from his high school teacher.

Why will people want to read your memoir?

They read reviews or learn in conversation that you have done an excellent job honoring your stories. They read the description on your back cover, whether online or in a bookstore, and sense they will benefit from your truth. They realize they will be entertained and informed. Your memoir focuses on a topic necessary to their lives. They want to read it because you have taken the time to craft a beautiful piece. For any of these examples, you need to paint a vivid picture of the theme and the threads you share.

From the beginning of my memoirs, I subtly attempt to tell my story. My solutions emerge once the reader comes to grips with the scenes. I don't hold back. I don't blame anyone. This process makes for good fodder.

Who especially will your memoir inform?

Your audience will appear when you conduct extra research, doing more than documenting your life. You can count on this impact when you write an educational piece, a how-to, or a self-help, crossover memoir. Everybody undergoes an experience that forms the core of their memoir, the hook.

- Have a theme larger than your life.
- Step back and evaluate what that entails for you.
- Use that main topic to your advantage.
- Write to it with all you have.

In my memoirs, I saw from the beginning how my themes could impact my advocacy work and wrote to that each time. I put myself in the shoes of those who walked with and before me and advocated for those who would come after me. Even in a dark place, my scenes take you to the truth.

Who will your memoir entertain?

- Those readers who find humor in life, despite their situation.
- Those who seek laughter and joy in life, even in the darkest times.
- Those who view life lightly and do not dwell on the negative.
- Those who realize everything that happens to us offers a lesson.

My memoir on domestic violence was a tremendous learning experience and an opportunity to look at myself in a way that was not all doom and gloom. I shared some of this eye-opening behavior and accepted the things I did in desperation that I could find humorous later.

What questions will your readers have about your story?

Readers' questions may range from, "Do you worry about retaliation?" to "How did you get the courage to write your stories?" Your answers will be enough. They will see how you molded your words together in your work. Whatever the question, be willing to answer it. They come to your event to hear you speak about your experiences and adventures. Give them what they want.

My book events have been fruitful. I encourage questions and read the nitty-gritty of the book at the event without "giving away the store." For example, to be a better presenter on love addiction, a topic not understood by many people, I've been extremely open in my presentation. They still ask questions.

What aspects of your story are most important to your readers?

You will answer this by looking at the threads you weave through your theme. These threads are the points in each chapter that impact your reader. Your writing purpose and your passion are essential to the reader. If you are emotional and moved by your story, they will be too.

I made my purpose clear in my memoir about my recovery from alcohol. I serve women searching for peace in their lives without alcohol. I unfolded stories of the people who helped me through my life change. I offered a hand to others by paying it forward. Several of my stories paint a picture of one woman helping another.

What aspects of your story will bore readers?

Expect anything unrelated to the presumed central theme to bore them. This includes trivia irrelevant to the book's overall goal about you or other characters. You can be sure to bore the reader if you use a lot of flowery descriptions that detract from what you are trying to show in a scene.

I was careful not to elaborate to the point of losing my stories when discussing the people in my early recovery. I edited the stories about sponsorship, meetings, and therapy. While critical, I needed to rein in the dialogue for the reader. Being succinct engages readers.

What do your readers value in a book?

- Quality writing, impeccable grammar, and punctuation.
- Exceptional organization and flow, piggybacked on relevant content.
- A hook at the beginning of the book and a teaser at the end of each chapter.
- The basics of a good novel.

Readers will thank you for giving them something of value they can take with them when they come to the end of the story.

I ensured my story of domestic violence went full circle, taking the reader back to where I wanted to be. After a devastating existence, I arrived at that destination but did not leave them guessing about what I needed to do to thrive.

What do your readers value in life?

They value many of the things you all do, or they would not be interested in your memoir. They have had similar experiences and aspire to how you handled them. After reading your work, their lives will change.

The response to my domestic violence story has been incredible. My readers deeply relate. By being brutally honest, I revealed what happened to me and my part in all of it. I sell that book three to four times more than my others.

What do you want your readers to know about you after reading your work?

You'll want them to know you're courageous, what you accomplished or lived through. With support, and by being authentic and honest in your storytelling, you show them the way.

People have told me my memoirs are read like a young woman's diary. I consider that a compliment. I have also heard the words brave and courageous when I speak to various audiences about my topics. To touch and change people is success to me.

How do you want your readers to feel when they read your memoir?

You want them to feel grateful their life has been more pleasant than yours or that they can have the life you have today despite what they have been through. You want them to feel more vital for reading your memoir and to experience something powerful so they can give you feedback on their transformation. You do not want the reader to feel alone.

Often, my readers tell me they learned more about my topics, such as love addiction or domestic violence, and now feel informed. They read the book looking for something else yet enjoyed it for what it added.

Do your readers want to laugh, cry, or both?

Rarely can a reader tolerate a book filled with only sadness and heartache. They don't necessarily want a book with only funny stories, either. That is not real life. Instead, combine both to create a memoir both palpable and enjoyable. You don't need to embellish the joy in some parts. Celebrate where it shows up naturally. Share the sadness as you recollect and take care to express it. Then the reader can relate to the sorrow and find the grace of the story.

My recovery is filled with stories of sadness and loneliness. They fill many chapters. The beauty of recovery and the joy of sobriety come through later as I share what happened over decades. I leave nothing to chance and show my warts to endear the reader.

Do your readers have a sense of humor?

They do if you do, or they appreciate your sense of humor if they do not. People are able to appreciate humor depending on what's going on in their lives. A book of stories can share laughter. It should not be filled with it.

In my first memoir, about my youngest sister's battle with cancer, I still found some humor. I remembered her wit and brought it out. Incredibly, she even found humor in her last days.

Do your readers typically look for a book like yours?

Most memoir readers have read this genre for some time. They appreciate real-life stories. They love finding stories to which they can personally relate. Books come in various categories, starting with:

- True memoir with a specific incident or situation.
- Complex memoir carrying research and historical information.
- Memoir on family history for legacy's sake.

I chose to write an accurate account focusing on a specific instance or situation in my life for all three of my memoirs:
- My sister's death from lung cancer and our relationship.
- My love addiction recovery and assault from domestic violence.
- My forty years of recovery from alcohol and my spiritual transformation.

I did a lot of research with the last two books. They are more complex in many ways. The topics are universal, but they are truly memoirs with a bit of legacy woven into the stories.

Where do readers find the books they read?

Readers quickly go to Amazon.com or other online websites, though those are not the only sources. Many readers want to meet the author, so they attend book festivals and book signings. Some choose based on the influence of reviews, friends, or their book club. The key is to be ready and visible in various places where readers can find you.

I give talks at book festivals, libraries, events, and book signings. My strategic plan for success involves face-to-face contact with my current and potential readers to elevate my author platform and book sales. I also carry out online marketing through social media.

What do you want your readers to say about your memoir?

"I could not put it down."
"You were so brave to write this."
You want readers to express openly how the book impacted their lives and how it has been cathartic for them too. If you want them to say something specific, ask subtly in the author

section at the back of the book. Requesting feedback, preferably online, brings the reader along with you.

I specifically ask for feedback on the author request page in my memoirs. Even though readers assume authors want feedback, I do not leave anything to chance.

Activity: Prepare for promotion

With your book's audience in mind, do the following:
1. Write a paragraph on why a customer would want to buy your book.
2. Identify the features and benefits (motivation) of your book.
3. List the features in one column and the benefits in the other.
4. Glean from these lists your audience's geographics and demographics.
5. Finally, develop the psychological reasons they will buy your book.

You are now able to prepare a starting promotion from this information.

15. Endless Homework

*Everybody talks about finding your voice.
Do your homework and your voice will find you.*

— Branford Marsalis, American saxophonist

Homework is a set of tasks a teacher assigns to be performed outside of a learning environment. The student must develop, devise, draw up, put together, concoct, arrange, and produce. Preparation is the action or process of making or being ready for use or consideration.

Given this definition, "endless homework" is a metaphor for authoring the book you imagine writing. The main difference between authoring and homework? We are not necessarily under the scrutiny of a watchful eye, at least initially. In most cases, writing is a lonely life. We live alone for a long time before we take on a writing partner, a critique group, or an editor.

To get good grades and advance in school, we know "practice makes perfect," whether learning a task or participating in a competition. Ditto with our writing. The more we write, the better we get, and the more we learn about writing, the better we become at the craft, increasing the possibility of becoming a respected author.

I realized after my first book how important writing is to me, so I continually strive to improve my skills. It makes no sense to stop learning after leaving school. As a writing student, I finish "endless homework" for my monthly critique group. I am eager to learn from successful memoirists and other writing professionals every time I attend a writers' conference or author talk. I strive to achieve the best possible book

I certainly do not think I know everything about writing memoirs even though I have been in this industry for more than twenty years. I am more than a senior citizen teaching a memoir writing workshop, while writing my fourth nonfiction book. New knowledge keeps me young.

My passion for writing memoirs is strong. I take this art very seriously and continue to discover my true purpose.

I want writers to answer these questions:

- How do they determine the hook, the teaser, and attention getter in their story?
- How do they find innovative ideas and new concepts?
- How do they communicate clearly, with a new spin on a familiar idea?
- How do they meet their writing goals?

Concepts and ideas

A key element for your book involves finding within your ideas one big concept that sticks in the reader's mind. Something untried. You want to tell your story in a unique way. This is how you will stand out in the sea of books in the memoir genre. Not to embellish your story or change it in any way—this encourages people to immediately take notice and keep reading. Your biggest challenge in writing memoir is expressing emotion. Get to know yourself.

This happens when you take the "what if" approach with your idea or concept. You step away from your story and look at it from the reader's point of view. If you do this often enough and never turn in a first draft to your critique group or your editor, you may rewrite it four or five times for improvement.

Memoirs focus on your introspection, your individual experiences, your families, and personal growth, and your transformation. A concept or big idea can appear when you take your memoir to the next level by going deeper into your psyche.

In *Sick as My Secrets*, I address my trajectory of alcohol and grief, and the loss of my spirit, as a blessing instead of a negative. I take the high road and use my story to strengthen women who carry shame and fear around alcohol. This approach fits the times. My memoir focuses on the rise of the disease in women and my desire to release the stigma of alcoholism. Recovery is a badge of courage, not a failure.

At least half of the time, women never recover due to shame. They hide in the shadows. I am grateful to be strong in my faith and believe the key is renewing my spirit by discussing it freely. This process is cathartic at the very least.

Thinking of the idea

So much of writing involves considering which ideas you will incorporate into your book. Writing the table of contents, mind mapping with a tree as your theme and branches as the threads, and brainstorming are all needed to foster those ideas and evolve with your writing. These critical concepts foster our learning about this craft throughout our writing careers.

As a curious person, I love Google, the dictionary, the thesaurus, and the library. I am willing to learn more about the benefits of artificial intelligence (AI), but I reluctantly learn and use it. Fortunately for me and my readers, I have an innate inquisitiveness about the unseen part of things. You may be that type of individual too. We find the things behind the scenes, the backstory, irresistible. To obtain the whole story, I research a person or place and stay in the creative world of books, plays, movies, and art. I want to know and remember all the details, not just those I initially recollect.

My "homework" to-do list for a fresh writing project consists of:

- Doing extensive online research.
- Taking a trip to the library for backup on universal topics.
- Scratching out ideas and sentences in a notebook.
- Piecing together my chosen concept in a couple of separate ways.
- Producing a handwritten rough first draft with no edits.
- Being willing to begin immediately.

The book's title may change slightly after my research. The basics remain the same. I create a rough outline and, from that, a first draft to determine each chapter's storyline. I may grow anxious and have after-thoughts about my stories over something I imagine. To begin, I look at how to define my journey with those stories: where I am from, who I married, or where I lived after I left home. To avoid writer's block, I take care of myself. I exercise and read to deal with emotional issues as they arise so as not to slow the creative process.

It is also important to not define yourself exclusively by your history—where you come from, circumstances of marriage and divorce, children, life and death, birth order, and how you feel about all of it. You can accept you are not "the house you grew up in." You are more than that little place in the world. However, the myths surrounding your birthplace do make for a better story. This attitude does not give that place power, but rather a jumpstart to a great concept and big idea. The key is to tune into the words, phrases, and sentences you write.

> *I grew up at the Straits of Mackinac at the north end of the Mackinac Bridge in St. Ignace, Michigan. It is located in the Upper Peninsula (UP) of Michigan, fifty miles south of the Canadian border. Two of the Great Lakes, Huron and Michigan, surround it. A truly picturesque place. Founded in 1671, this town has a long and colorful history.*
>
> *Snowbound and mystical in the dead of winter, St. Ignace grows vibrant and full of tourists in the summer. Approximately 3,200 people lived there when I graduated from high school in 1968. Due to the end of the baby boom, it has now shrunk to 2,200 people. There are no stoplights in this small town where you buy a ticket to the charming and quaint Mackinac Island.*
>
> *I could not wait to leave fifty-five years ago. Today, I yearn to return when the summer months come to call in Arizona. I am a cheerleader for Michigan and, especially, the UP. In other ways, I long ago moved on as I outgrew the area.*
>
> *Growing up on Graham's Point in a small house just up the hill from Lake Huron is for me, today, a paradise lost. When it was spring and the weather offered no more snow, we swam in the straits and watched the sailboats and ships pass by. Life was good.*

It held a different kind of beauty in the winter with the snow hanging heavy on the spruce branches and icicles glistening from the rooftops.

I find it hard to stop romanticizing Mackinac County when I write from my heart. Most memoirists experience this when writing about home. When I accept an assignment to write about my earlier life, I tell challenging stories, happy and sad. Romance comes in as it should, as it is impossible to keep it all the time. Life takes twists and turns, and it is far better to present the story both positive and negative. Your editor, writing partner, or readers will see through you if you do otherwise.

These ideas might help:
- Sort through your emotions when you check for romanticizing.
- See the bigger picture, the universal story.
- Ask yourself what your writing is trying to tell you and others.
- Envision how to write it so readers can move through it.

It is not an easy task to write an understandable memoir, so our words fully paint the depth of an experience. Although I have lived my stories, I can forget to include key points because they are obvious to me, but not to the readers. Emotions are the language of memoirs. You show your intentions through emotional details. Train the reader's mind's eye to find the heartbeat. After at least four rewrites, you can craft your story and produce an "A" paper.

Trusting the memory

One of the most asked questions in my memoir writing workshop is, "How do I trust my memory?" My answer is always the same: intuition and a belief in your stories. We are not reporters of the truth—we are storytellers. We show the life we lived in our own words. We are fulfilling an assignment for ourselves and our readers by sharing what we know and what we have learned.

Another question that pops up often is, "How do I write about people I love without betraying them?" My answer to that question is also easy: write what you recall and how it feels right for you. We all approach life differently. None of us can tell you how to do that in any other way but honestly. Believe in the power of the story.

I view my world very differently since my assault. It affected me more than any other event in my life. I needed to tell my story. I betrayed or slandered no one. It is the way I choose to live, both for my closure and healing and for the greater good. The information I shared holds true for others on the same path. I offer my truth and honor my faith.

In our memoirs, we impart what is going on with us now, even though we are writing about what happened in the past.

I am frequently asked, "How do I find my own voice?" My answer: listen to yourself while you read your work aloud. It will come naturally. By reading other memoirs, you will enhance your writing and develop your voice. Eventually, you will write with a loving heart and a humble spirit.

Before I did any memoir writing, I struggled with years of therapy and recovery. I learned much about myself, a fortunate exercise for both me and my readers. Because of those sessions and meetings, I project onto the world who I am and how I can be responsible for myself. What I say, do, and will do are important to me. I question myself before I write, to ensure my words are relevant, truthful, and helpful. I try to be interesting and humble.

Writing the memories

In this book, I share my perspective on writing memoirs with insights and discoveries. I impart my expertise so you can learn about yourself as a writer. The beginning of the book deals with the basics. I communicate my philosophy about writing throughout, which is critical to the book's overall appeal. Having lived the writer's life for more than twenty years, I feel comfortable sharing my stories and expertise.

When you write, be truthful. Do not apologize. People are hungry for real-life experiences, something I discovered while facilitating workshops on writing memoirs and talking about my books. Far more than I anticipated, readers yearn for another story to learn from, laugh with, and cherish.

Memoirs are more popular today than a decade ago. We must tell our stories to help us mend the disconnect in our society. Write. Authors who write in other genres are coming to memoirs—more every day. If you are one of those, welcome.

I only request you learn where to draw the line. Do not share specific details that could offend your readers, such as a violent or sexual encounter. You can share the illusion of what happened and still have an impact. Acknowledge that your reader has an imagination.

I write my memoirs with purpose. As mentioned, I talked about my abuser, but not by name. I gave him no power. I shared details about the night of the assault, including how I ended up in the emergency room, but not all the nitty-gritty details. The reader can read between the lines. They do not need to be there. I write vivid, not offensive, descriptions. I write to intrigue my readers to join me in the scene yet not be afraid. After thinking long and hard about what I will write, I put it out there. I proudly tell my story. I save all full disclosures for my therapy sessions.

Getting it right

Do your best to get it right when you accept an assignment or deadline. Do not worry about every word you write or stress over every scene discussed. Plant the dream in your heart to harness it. Do not lose sleep over your memoir writing. That action solves nothing. It certainly does not produce a good piece of work.

What can you do if you're afraid you have failed with your writing?

- Keep writing until you feel more comfortable.
- Show your work to a writing partner or critique group for their opinion.
- Pay an intellectual property attorney for an analysis.

It is not wise to take the attitude that you absolutely do not care what others think. You can care but not necessarily change your writing. Your draft encompasses only the beginning, not your final draft. You'll seek editing in all cases, so write it the way you want to write it. Protect your writing and your truth first and protect people later. This represents freedom for a memoir writer. Liberate yourself and put anxiety aside.

If you deal with issues similar to mine—love addiction, domestic violence, recovery, post-traumatic stress, grief, or spirituality—you are not alone. These issues affect a generous portion of our population. You will touch nerves, so consider yourself responsible for writing with accuracy and authenticity.

People buy my books for distinct reasons. I do not guess my reader's motives for reading my work. I deal with my truth head-on. I write about my experiences and finish the assignment given. My "endless homework" is to continue to author my stories and help others.

Retaliation

I have addressed this topic in other chapters, and it is worth reviewing again here. An often-posed question in my workshop is, "What obligation do I have to the dead?"

My answer comes easily: "They are gone, and you are here, ready to tell your story. They may or may not have known you would write your memoir, so make decisions honestly and speak for them. Do not look back. This approach will take you to peace."

Writing about my sister came easily. I loved her and still miss her deeply twenty-plus years later. I told her I planned to publish our story. Her battle with lung cancer and her courage and strength needed recording. I know she approves of the book. Her friends do too. I redid the cover and a dozen sections in the book in 2023 to honor her. The chapter I wrote on how I feel twenty years later is one example. The ache remains, just in another place. Grief has its phases but never really leaves me. It eventually settles in for the long haul.

I respected her in my first book and authored our story. I preserved her privacy and shared appropriately about her wit and courage while dealing with life challenges. I did not have to explain everything. We bonded together over shared battles. I enjoyed writing about someone I loved because, in the second memoir, I wrote about someone I resented and later forgave. These types of stories need sharing out in the world.

I used my natural humor in my second memoir to avoid retaliation. I chose not to be harsh. That is not me. I do not recommend using retaliation for effect in any story. It will not work for you, and your readers will see through you. Make yourself the joke. Play the devil's advocate. Be willing to stand up to those who dispute you.

I've had ugly people in my life. They taught me lessons about myself. If I do not want or need to write about the ugly ones, I do not. In the case of the abuser in my domestic violence story, I found it necessary. I prefer to write about those who have helped me.

I included more of that in my memoir on recovery and spirituality. While writing felt emotional and difficult at times, it has become more fulfilling now that I am at peace with myself. To have retaliated against anyone would have been harmful to my creativity.

I tell my stories because they are important.

Preparation

I ask my husband to read my chapters after I've completed three to five drafts. He is quite a good writer and also a published author. I trust him to give me valuable feedback. I ask him to look for my unique story and tell me what he learned from my pages. Consider seeking a writing partner or a critique group to start. I cannot express how valuable my critique group's feedback has been to me. I use about ninety percent of it and discard the other ten percent. Then I begin a three-round editing process of the entire manuscript with a professional editor as soon as possible. The editing part of the process takes thirty to forty-five days at a minimum.

Prepare mentally to turn your work over to an editor. Send your editor a clean copy. This action is paramount to your editing process and the flow of your final product.

As you complete this monumental task, ponder the following questions.

- Do the people you write about have psychological depth?
  - Their depth shows their traits and how you define them.
  - Determine their depth by understanding the genre, your voice, and the grammatical skills you possess to bring out their best and worst.
- Do you fully comprehend the scope of your memoir?
  - The scope is the area of your life addressed in this writing: the milestones, the events, the experiences, and what you want to deliver to the reader.
  - The scope also includes the goals, deadlines, features, and project tasks.
- What flashbacks should you use to add depth to your story?
  - Consider those that give your scenes power and allow you to ramp up the action.
  - Jump into the action, come back to a flashback, and insert it for effect.
- How will you use dialogue to provide a unique identity for you and others?
  - Accent your qualities and beliefs. Show us your self-image, self-esteem, and personality.
  - Integrate your life experiences and show unity and purpose with others.

- How do you allow the people in the story, and yourself, to overcome challenges?
  - Change your perception about the situation to see your growth and that of others.
  - Do not give up on the story. Write to the resolution.
- How well have you described the turning point that altered your life and that of others?
  - Evaluate what happened that caused a shift or change in your life.
  - Look for the specific moments when something came with monumental ease.
- How will you limit the use of narrative and increase your dialogue?
  - Show reality and emotion in your conversations.
  - Use strong, direct, useful words to make them count.
- How will you engage the reader from page one?
  - Punch up the first line by starting your story quickly.
  - Create tension immediately and use a strong commanding voice.
- How do you provide satisfactory resolutions to the challenges faced?
  - Identify the issues you show in your scenes and list the practical solutions.
  - Evaluate your options and work to understand the reader's reaction.

Activity: Homework

Make a list of twelve things you learned growing up in your hometown. Go back and narrow the list to three things. Write a line or two about each of them. Now select *only* one and write at least three paragraphs on that item.
Address the following questions:
- What have you learned about your hometown that is important to you?
- How did you learn this information?
- What surprised you about this knowledge?
- What, if anything, can you do about it?
- How can you use it in your writing?
- How forthcoming will you be?

16. Psychology of Storytelling

There are no friends as loyal as a book.

— Earnest Hemingway, American journalist and author

When writing a memoir, you must understand the psychology of storytelling and the differences in writing for self-healing versus personal development. Sometimes they are the same. Your work can be cathartic, not therapeutic. Heal first, then be courageous in your writing. Your development will follow and offer much to the reader.

We must use our experience in self-development when publishing books to help others and ourselves. In memoir/nonfiction, the reader seeks our wisdom, experience, and lessons learned. Use emotion to weave the delicate threads of your life. Make the most of the opportunity to explore the complexity of your human existence.

With each story, give the reader the narrative and the story. Summarize and describe your scenes, illustrating what you mean.

- Show the reader what happened through your mind's eye.
- Enable your reader to witness your experiences.
- Show the reader the truth in your scenes.
- Bring the action.

The readers press us for the deeper meaning of our experiences in the moment, a wider view.

My business career spans more than forty years, exclusively in the Phoenix metropolitan area. Ironically, I was not seeking a future in business when I moved here in 1976. I enrolled at Arizona State University to study psychology and sociology. Life happened. I took classes, acquired a real estate license, and began collaborating with my former husband in a realty office during a fast upswing in the housing market.

This decision caught me in a sales career. I did not initially work in realty sales full time; I attended college too. I did not love selling and felt pressured to do it. My husband needed my help with his real estate business. I learned to sell for the wrong reasons and felt disgruntled about the situation. I wanted a career in a completely different field. That did not happen for almost twenty years.

Storytelling, a universal experience across cultures and throughout history, allows writers to paint a verbal picture. The psychology of storytelling highlights a built-in need as humans for empathy and support.

For no apparent reason, memoir readers often set aside their lives to learn about yours. They read memoirs for the topic, the author, the overall theme, the joy of learning, the reward of self-healing, or the thrill of success. They take on your goals and seek to understand your dilemma. They imagine how you felt, sympathize with you, and attempt to walk in your shoes. Your readers experience your emotions and begin to connect with your experience.

We are all human. We share fundamental ways to cope and respond to life's events. We all harbor a dark side. The hero's journey runs deep in every culture. We want to cheer for the hero. While difficult, the fear the hero feels when facing danger can also serve as the greatest motivator.

Readers want a successful conclusion. They want to see victory for the hero. They seek human transformation when they read memoirs. Our job as writers involves the creation of meaningful story events for the readers. Our story requires an arc, peaking at an upturn toward the resolution.

Humans need stories. The themes and threads emerge from this realization. Your readers will better understand how people and the world work through your experiences.

Help them understand by:
- Giving them a solid structure from which to begin.
- Showing them a storyline they can follow.
- Making them aware early on of your timeless themes.
- Using rhetorical questions to keep them turning the pages.

Readers engage your story by asking themselves why the characters did what they did, the universal question of the memoir. The psychology of story is at work then. Why people function as they do fascinates and confounds readers, so capitalize on what you've experienced and tell the story in detail with emotion.

You have two choices with your reader: to keep your distance, be aloof, and less threatening; or to become familiar and endearing. I am sure you know which way to go.

To become familiar, find your comfort zone with the following:
- Smells, sights, and sounds that describe your scenes.
- Mannerisms and behaviors unique to you.
- Aliveness in your story played out in action.
- Presence in the story, not outside looking in.

The structure of your story is paramount to your success. If you are producing a book series, maintain the structure, especially if it works for you. Your reader will become familiar with the empathy you want to achieve. Pull your readers in with conflict and immediately adjust the scenes so they feel like real life. Use suspense and secrets. The reader wants to find the answers to the questions. They will keep reading to do this.

Readers live vicariously through your story. They take on your goals, feel what you feel, know what you know, and observe you making important choices and decisions. Sometimes they feel curious. Your story can ignite a change in your reader if you understand the psychology behind telling a story. Your goal remains to kindle your reader's delight and enjoy your work, regardless of the personal impact on them.

The economy stayed healthy for about seven years during my first years in the real estate business. In the early 1980s, though, the interest rates began to rise and the usury law changed. Homebuyers feared the economy meant interest rates on mortgages had no lid.

I decided the resale end of the business was not for me. I interviewed four builders to sell new homes in a subdivision. Eventually, I joined a large national homebuilder as their first female salesperson. That was an interesting time. Fourteen men made up the sales force, and none of them relished me joining the team. I ignored their sexist remarks and actions. I persevered in spite of their unfair and rude behavior. I was determined.

To outsell all the sales associates by a sizable percentage, I sometimes worked seven days a week. I never looked back. By the end of my second year, the company nominated me as Rookie of the Year for the Arizona Homebuilders Association and Salesperson of the Year for the company. I was obsessed with the challenge. With this recognition and a healthy bank account, my social life suffered. I continued with new home sales for more than seven years. I paid the price with my health and spiritual well-being, particularly when I manipulated potential homeowners. Next, I focused on resales and brokered mortgages.

The end came when the economy turned, the bubble burst, and an economic downturn occurred. I used scare tactics to get people to buy houses. The interest rate climbed and had no ceiling. An eighteen percent interest rate on a mortgage was a hard sell. Every day was a difficult sales day.

I became shamefully good at scaring people. "The rates could go higher, like in Canada," became my mantra.

A colleague drafted a story profiling me and my success selling in a challenging market. The article appeared in our corporate national newsletter.

After twenty-five years in the industry, I felt exhausted.

Emotional core

The story's emotional core meets the expectations of the reader when it grasps their attention and, at the same time, makes the story timeless and meaningful. If you go deep, your work will be heartfelt. The core is more than the story's action—it encompasses deeper truths. By echoing with familiarity or causing a startling realization, these truths reassure the reader they can identify with you.

The emotional core of your story consists of the following story elements:
- How you felt.
- What you experienced.
- What you struggled with and the consequences.
- The emotional connections you have with others.

These emotional connections could lead to concern about the story's outcome or how to deal with the story's conflict. Your reader may empathize with you, given the undeserved misfortune or injustice you experienced.

Stories may emerge about how you survived or transformed after putting yourself in jeopardy, or how you built your character and became likeable and funny. You've become an expert.

The emotional core of your story relates to what you experienced and all the joy and heartache that went along with it.

Your lessons learned can share:
- What you learned from your mistakes.
- Your hard-won truths.
- The story's insurmountable odds.
- Something the reader can care about.

When you reveal your story in detail, your readers will walk side by side with you. They become part of the story. They will see where you deserve justice, freedom, peace, redemption, and a good life. They will relate to you if you give them solid, honest answers.

To unravel more, ask yourself:
- Is there a bigger piece to the story?
- Is there a deeper emotional core not yet revealed?
- What are the stakes for these revelations?
- What dramatic and emotional conflict am I willing to share?

You can be proud of your work by telling the story and being open. You create a powerful story when you open the door to an experience of compassion and change. By using the universal emotions of pain, desire, fear, and yearning, you prepare the reader to relate to your story.

Do not shy away from heavy topics. Allow your emotions to be visceral and primal. Take on topics like abandonment, rejection, grief, fear, anger, or sadness. Share the effect of a nurturing friendship, the beauty of a good friend. The reader realizes a human moment once they know the story and support you. They feel enlightened.

By remaining vulnerable as we write, by staying at the center, you raise the stakes and let go of what has held you back. Your work might even stay with the reader, "haunt" the reader if you will, after your story concludes. Be courageous. Try using sibling rivalry, loyalty, or hard truths about your family. Their reaction is in the stars. Whatever happens is meant to be.

The turning point in my real estate career came after struggling in a difficult economy. My social drinking became daily drinking. My personality, work ethic, and approach to business all changed. My attitude slipped—rarely positive. I tried to chase that elusive dream of yesterday's success. Eventually, a homebuilder terminated my position. This moment humbled me and forced me to look hard at what I was doing. While the economy contributed to my unemployment, I burned out on the business. I no longer desired a sales position.

I sought out a therapist and made substantial changes in my life. I set personal goals, including recovery. I moved from Tempe to Scottsdale and rented a small condominium. By going to therapy weekly and staying sober, I gained a clearer picture of what I wanted to do with my life. I worked as an overqualified realtor assistant for four years and went to graduate school at night to finish a master's degree in organizational management.

Emotional core stories feel genuine, not empty. They tell it like it is with their honesty and values. With frankness and openness, you can share your worries and allow your readers access to your rawest, most painful emotions. When you are authentic, you deal with loneliness and anger in a straightforward manner.

When you thoroughly use the following, your themes connect to your passion.

Work these as goals:

- Be raw and vulnerable. Author the timeless story of your life.
- Have a vision. Write with this psychology in mind.
- Plan to write genuinely. Do not see yourself failing.
- Become a writer in your mind's eye.
- Think, *This is who I am,* and write unabashedly.
- Have a special pen, notepad, laptop, journals, or other device nearby.
- Function as a successful writer by presenting yourself confidently.

The physical and technical parts will follow. You cannot just visualize. You must act out what you have learned and read other memoirs to write yours. Feel the thrill of being a writer by creating a place to write and printing "writer" on your business card.

Try these ideas to get you going each day:

- Do not ask for financial success. Focus on creating valuable writing.
- Ask for personal success, including respect from your readers.
- Visit other author events and observe their behavior.

- Become emotionally involved in the psychology of writing.
- Go forth in faith that you will bring your mind, body, and spirit with you.
- Choose what makes you smile, what will give your idea power.

While pursuing my graduate degree and working on my thesis, I joined the Human Resources Network and met interesting people. I learned how to update my résumé and practiced my thirty-second pitch. I kept a good attitude, and when asked what I wanted to do with my advanced degree, I was ready to reply. Although it was an emotional roller coaster ride, I stayed upbeat despite often feeling great sadness. It took a lot of work to make a career change at midlife.

I was a fallen star working my way back while out of my element. I was not on top then, so it was quite an adjustment. I had to make it work for me. No one asked how I was doing and how the job search was going. Making that career change was important to me, so I kept going.

If, at times, you feel insecure about storytelling and putting yourself out there, list everything bothering you and write about those items in your journal pages. Ask yourself why each item is an issue for you and what you can do about it. You help your writing by creating this list of resolutions and solutions and letting go of the items that do not serve you.

Psychology permeates your storytelling. You stay motivated by what is possible. Meditate on what you want and envision it with conviction. This will drive you to act immediately. By moving forward, even for a brief period, you untie your hands to write more often.

Keep the reader in mind

Care deeply about your theme and honor the times you can share your expertise.

- Do not be bossy. Refrain from allowing that behavior into your work.
- Remember, giving knowledge requires sensitivity. Your readers need a ray of hope. They need to laugh and see your softer side while you share your expertise in the narrative. But more importantly, they need your humanity, and they need it with grace.
- Do not anger your readers with a rigid idea that may deaden their emotions. This is key in your "show, don't tell" approach.
- Care about your readers. Then they reciprocate with mutual respect.

Memoir uses both subtle and specific means to bring truths and themes to light. Take this seriously. Step away from the pulpit or the podium. Avoid too persuasive a tone. Leave those words for an appendix if they need to appear.

I questioned whether my two decades in the real estate business would transfer to a corporate training position. The career shift seemed risky. While in graduate school, I lived in an apartment for the first time in twenty-five years. The anxiety, fear, and frustration of it all put me on an emotional roller coaster. I taught part-time at an area community college, and later at the local university, while starting my home-based training business. My timing worked. I used the economy in reverse as inside trainers were being let go and freelance trainers like me were being hired when needed.

It was not easy. I experienced difficulties for more than four years, teaching, training, and consulting. When I worked from home, my business life dominated all my time. I now had a computer, an email, and a cell phone, which put me at risk of burning out again. I needed to start enjoying the day.

While I searched for an easier way to move forward, I stayed close to my recovery life and those friends who had been there for me. Teaching proved to be the hardest, least paying, and most rewarding job I have ever loved.

You will touch your readers' hearts by using a light touch with your themes, not hellfire and brimstone. Tell them the truth about your work to help them learn the universal truths of your stories and experiences, and the connection to who you are and what you show.

The psychology of storytelling for your reader relies on your skill to:

- Talk about your theme and the underlying message.
- Tell readers what inspires you and enlighten them.
- Use scenes to show your story's narrative arc, its structure and shape.
- Boldly give them your prominent theme.
- Ease them into your view.
- Walk the reader gently, yet forcefully, through your stories. The meaning of your words must embody the storyline.
- Show how these moments resonate with you.
- Review these last thoughts on the psychology of storytelling:
- Do not state your theme directly. Respect the reader.
- Tell us what whispers to you, what you must write.
- Examine how other authors do this.
- Ponder the values and beliefs of others around you.

Where and when we write matter. A beautiful and comfortable workspace is invaluable. Enjoyment of your writing life means making it your own. To be a happy and content writer and author, you must allow things to flow. Show what is happening with the words on the page, the submission you sent out, or your last event. This is now your writing life. When you act each day to move two steps forward, and delay gratification in other areas, you achieve your writing goals. The feeling of satisfaction can be therapeutic.

It is important to let go of whether you write from your left or right brain, or a combination of both. It takes all kinds of writers to succeed. The right brain finds ideas and drafts the stories. The left-brain researches and produces a book proposal or marketing plan.

Add these to your repertoire:
- Honor the cycles you must go through.
- Stop feeling guilty if you take time off from your writing to flesh out an idea.
- Take care of yourself and be who you are as a writer.
- Genuinely love your creative expression or start on another project.

We all want the same thing, but we arrive at the finish line in multiple ways. You will fall in love with your project if you let it happen. There is nothing worse than grinding out pages for the sake of a deadline when you are not in love with your idea.

Psychologists will tell you that receiving inspiration and motivation from people, objects, and photos will change the brain and the way you think. By choosing what makes you happy and what you believe will work for you, you celebrate your progress. As you stay positive and work toward your publication goals, all of this will be reflected in your manuscript. Your readers deserve this effort, so reward yourself with a treat when you accomplish these steps.

When you develop relationships with writing friends and share your pages or chapters, they will applaud your success and listen and suggest when there are rough spots. They walk the same path and want to succeed and win.

Activity: Writing Prompt.

Select one of the following starter words and write with one of your stories in mind, preferably one you have not used in the past:
1. Fear, anger, pain, loss, hope, love, peace, friendship, or connection.
2. Set a timer and write with fierce abandon for ten minutes.
3. If you want to write longer, do so.
4. Review your work twenty-four hours later to discover what it is you really wrote.

17. Why a Writing Coach?

The quality of a person's life is in direct proportion to their commitment to excellence, regardless of their chosen field of endeavor.

— Vince Lombardi, American football coach

When we first started Brooks Goldmann Publishing Company in 2005, we offered consultations to guide writers and authors through the maze of independent publishing. We continue that practice today with a team of editors, designers, and ghostwriters. Over time, however, many requests came in for individual guidance and added a writer's coach option to our company.

I referred people to outside coaches for a while, but realized early on how much I would enjoy working with writers one-on-one. After I taught at the college and university level for fifteen years, my writing career was going full speed ahead. Prior to that, I consulted with many women in business. I excelled and felt valued. I saw the need for a writing coach in so many areas of the writing process. I made a conscious decision to help those writing memoir or nonfiction books. For other genres, we continued to refer to editors on our vendor list.

My coaching credentials included participating in a critique group for twenty years and writing four books, three of which have been published and one to be published soon. I have now taught my memoir-writing workshop for more than ten years, at least a dozen times a year, while consulting with authors and writers for almost fifteen years. Coaching one-on-one feels natural.

Managing my women writers' club, the Scottsdale Society of Women Writers, taught me a lot about what aspiring writers want and need. Owning a publishing company has given me endless experiences to coach writers into success. By attending writers' conferences and festivals each year and participating in book events, I gain insight into how writers and authors feel about writing, who needs a coach, and who doesn't.

What does a writing coach do?

- Guides you through all phases of the writing process.
- Determines a workable schedule for all involved.
- Develops a specific and detailed writing plan with you.
- Organizes the project with your help.
- Remains available for face-to face meetings, emails, text messages, and phone calls.
- Critiques/proofreads your pages or a chapter each month.
- Mentors you to reach new heights.

Once I came to understand what separates coaches from editors, I knew I wanted to be a writing coach. The editor works with writing technique and semantics. The coach focuses on getting it right by seeing the big picture. The process of developing the idea, the first draft and the polished draft, has its difficulties. Submitting the work to an editor or coach supports and encourages the writer.

Coaching resembles more of a personal, tutoring relationship. I find a great deal of intrinsic value in it and gain a feeling of accomplishment when the writer's book comes to fruition. Once the writer recognizes the value of my expertise and sincere encouragement, trust is established. This is a win-win situation for both me and the writer.

A writing coach relates to your struggles by offering up solutions to your challenges. A good coach holds you accountable in a firm and gentle way, so sticking to goals and completing the project is fun. Together, you and the coach identify these goals, write them down, visualize their success, and prioritize them.

By being more than a guide to produce a book, a coach recognizes skillful writing and works with you to maintain your best with each page. They encourage you to stay committed and focused on your objectives (what to do) and strategies (how to do it) needed to reach your ultimate goal—to publish. The coach and the writer partner to plan and organize a workable structure. They overcome challenges that interfere, either at a personal or business level, and handle them quickly. You continue to improve your writing.

How does the coach help you?

- Keeps you focused.
- Provides perspective and guidance.
- Stays objective about your work.
- Mentors you and provides training in various aspects of writing.
- Eases your frustration through listening and conversation.
- Helps you get and remain organized with tasks and goals.
- Supports your ideas and finds value in them.
- Encourages the writer and builds confidence.

As I guide them through the writing process to publication, my coaching clients benefit. By admitting earlier rather than later you need a writing coach, you step onto your path of success with your best foot forward.

During the partnership, you develop the book's premise early and discuss the concept and ideas thoroughly. These actions eventually result in your goals. Through interviews, we learn about your writing experiences and how you can use any writing expertise you already possess to propel these elements with your creativity. We immediately work to find the heart of your content, seeking out the emotional beats of your story and how to use them constructively.

We want you to become a better writer, produce a polished work, and publish. These are not lofty goals. To obtain them, they often need the support of a kind and encouraging confidant. That is the job of the writing coach.

Suggested first-round goals:

- Learn early the fundamentals of writing a memoir/nonfiction manuscript, your stories, your truth.
- Understand the genre, one piece of your life, an experience, or a happening.
- Learn the process of writing memoir—not a chronological legacy, but a story that unfolds with conflict and suspense.
- Develop a structure of scenes, dialogue, and the arc of the story, similar to fiction writing.
- Produce an outline and a tentative table of contents to guide your ideas.
- Do research analysis, interview people, and revisit places to pull back long-hidden memories.
- Set attainable and realistic goals. Write them down and visualize them.
- Get organized. Use mind mapping, poster boards, flash cards, files, and journals.
- Visualize a completion date. Mark it on a calendar and make plans.
- Know the road to publication. Learn as much as you can on your own.

Other suggestions for the partners:

- Sign an agreed-upon, open-ended contract, approved by witnesses.
- Determine monthly fees and stay on schedule.
- Send and receive payments in advance of meetings.
- Work toward an ongoing relationship of trust.
- Do what you say you'll do.
- Respect each other's views.
- Practice good listening skills.
- Meet face-to-face two times per month/every other week. Be consistent.
- Meet for a minimum of one hour. Respect the time.
- Seek fresh ideas at each meeting. Come with an open mind.
- Allow unlimited emails each month. Be respectful.
- Take phone calls/text messages and keep them on the topic at hand.

What's next?

- Set a detailed schedule and specific goals for at least a year.
- Provide an extensive questionnaire to establish your wants, needs, and initial plans.
- Prepare an advanced outline to determine the manuscript's topic, theme, and threads.
- Discuss any anticipated obstacles or challenges and seek solutions.

We begin with a free in-person "get to know you" consultation. A phone call suffices, if necessary, or a meeting online. At this meeting, I learn about you and your project, and you learn about me and my credentials.

We spend our introductory coaching session targeting specific needs, wants, and goals. We also draw up a specific plan and schedule for our ongoing relationship. We begin to develop a personal relationship, if we don't already have one, by asking as many questions as we need to move forward. We work toward unparalleled trust with each other and discuss what we hope to accomplish. If the writer is holding back any pertinent information, he/she will open up at this time.

Prior to the meeting, the writer answers the following questions and submits them to the coach:

- What are you working on currently?
- Do you have anything written or revised?
- What are the challenges and struggles you foresee?
- Are you able to be flexible with your current commitments?
- Will you be okay or overwhelmed with feedback?
- What do you want to accomplish?
- Are you focused on going forward?
- When do you want to start?

What are the benefits of a writing coach?

- Supporting you in many ways, including private tutoring, manuscript critique and evaluation, and ongoing encouragement.
- Accountability for you, and assurance you are always responsible for your writing project.
- An individualized touch, a sincere relationship of friendship.
- Less costly than an editor to start things and move forward.

- Shared expertise to help you learn the writing process.
- An objective view of the research needed to supplement the personal stories and anecdotes.

My personal goal is always to share my unique gifts as a coach and writer and to support you to experience success. My business goal is to jumpstart your creativity and help you connect with your authentic self by sharing my previous passion projects and learning about yours.

By expanding your perception of what a written manuscript looks like and what it can be, I help you dive deeper into areas that will strengthen your work. Finally, we continue to take a hard look at what is important to your theme and learn even more about you so you can be brave in your writing.

What kind of support do you need?

A writing coach can be extremely useful to you especially if you are a first-time writer, are entering a new genre, or want to learn more about a genre and hone your craft. The coach is there to guide you through the process of achieving all the goals you've set, and those suggested by the coach. A coach encourages and helps you break through any experience of writer's block. By issuing monthly or weekly critique pages and timely constructive feedback, a coach will support you. Shared accountability builds a strong partnership. Taking this relationship to the next level opens things up for you to develop advanced writing skills and clever techniques so your manuscript can stand out. All of these lead to the preparation of the book proposal, final critique for the editor's review, essential steps toward publication, and the support needed to take the book to fruition.

18. Writing Nonfiction

> *I still believe writing nonfiction is the most important literature to come out of the second half of the 20th century.*
>
> — Thomas Clayton Wolfe,
> a major American novelist of his time

To write memoir is to write nonfiction. When working in the memoir genre, ask yourself why you want to write and what you want to say. So much of what you produce will emerge from your inspiration and experience. However, research is also necessary.

Ask yourself if you can be an instrument for change with your words. Answer these questions in your planning journal:

- Am I willing to share my experience openly?
- Is being an advocate part of who I am?
- Is my purpose with this memoir to help educate, entertain, or inform others?
- What goals do I have for those who will read my memoir?
- Will writing nonfiction be cathartic for me?
- Will my current books or articles compliment or help this new work?
- Am I willing to say what matters to me?
- Have I had therapy first to help better manage the "hard stuff?"

I designed all three of my memoirs to help others. This has always been my purpose. I keep this mission statement in the forefront of my mind when I work. My objectives and strategies are my plan of action. With my outline, picture board, and mind-map (the tree and branches discussed earlier), I stay on track. This process helps me start each time I sit down to write.

When organizing your manuscript, the objectives point to your goals for the chapter, and the strategies spell out the steps you'll take to achieve them. When properly thought out, these deliver valuable information while also sharing with the readers what you feel.

In the very beginning, ask yourself if your story, or stories, grab the audience, hook them in, and are unique to you. Your message must be strong. Proficient writing is not enough. Your readers need the whole package of hooks, arcs, scenes, and dialogue to keep turning the page. Your passion for writing this memoir must come from your heart and soul, not only exist as a lot of words on the page with no emotion.

Ask yourself these ten critical questions:
1. What moves me?
2. How do I show what happened?
3. How do I prove the connection to the reader?
4. How do I give solutions to improve lives?
5. Will I share my soul?
6. What is my story's *yin* and *yang*, the cause and effect?
7. What critical solutions and lessons will I deliver?
8. Do I have a conclusion or wrap-up the reader can live with?
9. What takeaways will come from reading my memoir?
10. Whose voice do I need to represent?

With nonfiction, and especially memoir, we often tell stories for the underdog, the voiceless, or the less unfortunate—those who want to relate to what has happened to *us*. They yearn to relate. They may be in a comparable situation looking for answers.

This occurred with my memoirs. For instance, by receiving countless emails after my talks about grief, I saw the need to produce my own grief workshop.

The reader is enlightened by reading scenes and dialogue that illuminate what makes you who you are and how you have grown from your experiences. Honor your audience by being credible, trustworthy, and believable. Memoir writing is not about you, even though you write about yourself. It is meant for the reader to find answers and learn from your experience.

My first tip: Do your homework.

Preparation is paramount to your memoir's success. The importance of research in nonfiction/memoir cannot be overstated.

Journal on the following:
- Where and how will I search on the internet?
- Will I read books, articles, or blogs?
- Am I willing to keep journals for reflection?
- Will I research by using primary (firsthand) and secondary (secondhand) sources?
- Am I willing to do my homework to improve my memoir?

The above list describes secondary research, already published. The primary research includes face-to-face or phone interviews, observations, experiments, and casual conversations, to learn more. You don't need to commit to use everything you accumulate. Just stay focused on the goal at hand. Be methodical. Remind yourself you have a vision, a big picture for your writing. Your authentic self, in a particular incident, setting, or experience, becomes the umbrella over your chapters.

Be sure to have a vision for your success to stay motivated. By doing your research and studying your topic's history, you will structure your manuscript well. For example, I consider myself an authority on the topic of grief, having experienced it deeply at an early age. I am well read on the subject. I analyzed at least six books covering various aspects of grief. Before embarking on my first memoir about losing my sister, I attended four different workshops on the topic. I realized there were no shortcuts. I had to treat it similarly to fiction, with a lot of planning and organization. I looked to thoroughly understand grief and my relationship with it before I wrote.

To start my second memoir about love addiction and domestic violence, I took copious notes at workshops and group meetings. For me, these two topics overlapped. I experienced them simultaneously, which was difficult because of the extreme stress involved in a domestic violence relationship. Love addiction had lived in me all my life. I grew up yearning for attention and affection.

I chose to be responsible to those who would read my story by keeping my journal alive, writing on the side while living life. By immersing myself this way, I set the story free. I am now considered an expert in these topics. I have been there and done that. In therapy, I learned about myself, working through the trauma from an assault and otherwise. I shared my wisdom with my readers, and those who hired me to speak on the topics.

My knowledge on these topics came from a lot of published research and expert speakers. It took ten years after my domestic violence and assault experiences to go beyond journal writing and research love addiction. Very few talked about this difficult topic at the time.

I embarked on this memoir only after I was far enough away from those violent incidents and felt ready. To gain a clear perspective, I needed to analyze everything I'd experienced with love addiction in my life. I carried a notebook with me for a full decade and wrote in it whenever I had an insight or experience. These notes guaranteed I saw things clearly in my memoir.

With my third memoir, I wrote in depth about my four decades in alcohol recovery. I listened to people in recovery and asked a lot of questions before putting pen to paper. I kept records of what I saw and felt at recovery meetings, seminars, and conferences and was mindful of my thoughts as I wrote in my journal. By recording my feelings and emotions, and practicing mindfulness, I went to the heart of the story.

Consider the following questions:
- What gnaws at me in the night?
- Will I truthfully write from a place of anger or frustration?

- Am I willing to deal with trauma or social injustice?
- What do I need to be able to write about a crisis?

The emotional beats you hear in your head and feel in your heart are your inner voice. It's talking to your soul. Do not silence those beats. Pay attention, listen to your subconscious. I read ferociously on the topic of recovery. I welcomed all the ideas coming from within me. I spoke about my story to private groups who had similar experiences. I trusted myself and the messages I heard in my head.

My goal was, again, to be an expert, to learn everything I could to become an authority. Nonfiction is all about helping readers comprehend their life story by relating to ours. In memoir, you share your stories while learning about yourself, understanding what happened and why, and discovering the lessons from those events.

You finish your research with a follow-up plan. You must be eager to let the writing happen and not force the writing or any issue until it is ready to express itself. If you are aware of this, you will confirm the statements and ideas you convey in the manuscript.

My second tip: Consider the voice and structure of your memoir.

With nonfiction/memoir, you create the structure you prefer while also relying on ideas you encounter from research sources, including other memoirs. There is no definitive way to lay out a memoir. A chronological format is often used but is not a requirement. You may hook the reader with a strong attention-getting piece and go back to the beginning later. The main thing to remember is what motivated you to begin this memoir in the first place. Be mindfully aware and curious about what is best for you. If you are clear in your vision, you can transfer that to the reader and expand it.

Whether tragedy or success, desire for transformation, or a spiritual awakening or rebirth, something pushed you to complete this book. Involve all your senses. Pay attention to your subconscious, for that is your soul and a large part of your voice. Keep the faith and don't doubt yourself. Write, write, and write more.

Analyze what first interested you to go in unexpected directions. Ask:
- What is distinct about my life and theme?
- What is my book's concept?
- What do I need to do to reach my goals?
- What will I do differently from others?
- Will I paint a picture for a reader with my words?
- Will I harness distinct subject matter?

Memoir expands one experience or elaborates on a slice of life. While mindfully aware of who you are, you can come alive with your stories. Check to be sure you are clear with your goals by reviewing your story board, your mind map, or both.

My third tip: Set up your writing with a specific approach that illustrates its originality.

It is powerful to read other memoirs, but in the end, do not confine or alter your voice. You will find yours by listening within. The five W's of reporting—the who, what, when where and why (plus "how")—can be helpful, but do not pigeonhole yourself with this format.

Give yourself a workable timeline after you write your outline. This is the first step toward success. Emulate others who offer outlines on how to place deadlines for various aspects of your plan. Honor what you read or find in your research. Most importantly, let this work speak from your voice, and with the structure and format of your choice.

Reflect on these final questions in your journal:
- Why would anyone care if I authored this book?
- Will this work hold the interest of my ideal reader?

19. The Author Interview

When you're interviewing someone, you're in control. When you are being interviewed, you think you are in control, but you're not.

— Barbara Walters,
American broadcast journalist and personality

Several years ago, and the day before the Tucson Festival of Books, a local Tucson radio station interviewed me. This was not the first time I had been interviewed about my writing life, and as before, I enjoyed the process.

To prepare, the interviewer had read excerpts from a couple of my books. She asked the following questions:

How did you evolve into a memoir writer?

My journey is unique. As a perfectionist for most of my life, I could not imagine telling all my truths or writing them down for public criticism. Yet, today, that is what I do.

Though I began writing early on, the memoir concept arose when my sister became terminally ill and I vowed to tell her/our story. Writing and telling my stories helped me make sense of my chaotic life and heal. My memoirs tell the story of my evolution and my purpose to help others.

As a young person, I worried frantically about looking like an idiot. By writing in a diary, I hid those thoughts where no one, not my parents nor my three sisters, could read them. I carried forward the practice of keeping a journal long before it became fashionable.

Since then, writing memoirs has shown me that being vulnerable and bold, while baring my soul, is the way to share myself and help others. My purpose in life, with all my experiences, good and challenging, shapes me. Leaving my innermost thoughts and ideas on paper, instead of only in the therapist's office or a recovery room, gives me a feeling of usefulness.

Even though memoir writing can be painful at times, the freedom to deliver a clear storyline to the reader makes it enticing. Revealing deeply about domestic violence and love addiction in my second memoir became the backbone for my third memoir. My core stories centered around those two topics, plus recovery and spirituality.

Writing them helped me develop the techniques I'm sharing with you in this book. I humanized my stories and spoke from the heart. The vivid scenes and strong dialogue brought my stories to life. By being brutally honest about my behavior, how deep-seated those issues had become, I told the stories with fierce abandon and lured the reader to turn the page.

My personal reflections backed up my purpose to help others, especially to be of service to women. They took me to an even deeper level about who I am and what I am about.

Did you ever feel you shared too much?

No. I shared what needed to be said. The stories around my abuser are relevant. The stories attached to my time in jail and the battles with the courts are too. That vulnerable energy gives purpose to the action. I had to openly address all the trials and tribulations of drinking, quitting drinking, staying sober, and learning about myself.

In memoirs, you must be authentic and genuinely bare your soul. I committed to that idea early on and did not retreat. By dramatically showing many of my experiences with alcohol, my words played well for those seeking help for themselves or others. I immersed myself in recovery even more by reading books written by other women in recovery. My main goal to develop as a professional authority on the subject took priority.

These books could not be subtle. They had to authentically portray my story for the reader. They would not be impactful or helpful if I held back. I had to be my own sleuth, finding the underlying cause of the real story.

How did you start writing?

It happened early in my life and evolved into a need to do it. Although I could have been a better writer in high school, I was enthusiastic. My English teacher loved me for it and supported me with extra time and attention. Today, I remember her more than any other teacher. Writing has been within me all my life.

When I read, I want to write. When I hear a speaker, I want to speak and write about what I heard and felt. It's who I am and what I am about today. By growing more enthusiastic about my writing with every life experience, I have more stories to tell.

I learned early in life writing is generous. Nobody talks back to you. It is your voice, your way. When you journal, you don't have to justify what you want to say. You can write for freedom of expression.

Where I grew up in Mackinac, on Michigan's Upper Peninsula, we had a small-town library and a high school library. We did not have a bookstore. Only when I went away to college did I experience a local bookstore in the downtown area of Marquette, near Lake Superior. Later that year, I visited a giant bookstore in Detroit, The Big Bookstore. In awe of what they had to offer, I promised myself that, someday, I would author a book of my own and see it in a bookstore.

My stories speak for themselves. I tell them as they are, with no trepidation, from my heart and soul. I don't blame anyone for what happened to me. I acknowledge my journey. It sets me free to be the writer I am today. I know what I remember thinking and experiencing at the time. That is the story I tell.

What did you write before books?

As a businesswoman, I wrote business-related content, either for my company's newsletter or an industry publication. Many articles featured soft-skill topics, such as time management, team building, public speaking, personal success, or stress management. My career experiences, and what I learned from them, guided me in my writing and speaking career.

For more than twenty years, I worked in various capacities in real estate, a pressure cooker career. Although I won many awards and achieved Salesperson of the Month, Rookie of the Year, and Salesperson of the Year, I did not love the business. I was obsessed with the money and the recognition. I needed to catch up on what mattered.

To write from my heart and soul, and to serve others, meant transitioning from that place of self-centeredness to a position of higher meaning.

I realized I loved the English language, constructing words and sentences. I enjoyed sorting my problems in my journal. My writing helped me heal. I found solace and peace in some small way through writing.

After being assaulted, I drafted detailed stories for my group therapy sessions about what happened to me as if I were reliving a movie script. This supported my grief journey and helped me release anger. I held the diaries from my younger life in my subconscious. Coupled with my more recent journals, the writing came freely.

Due to several missteps in my personal life, and some circumstances out of my control, my real estate career changed drastically. I moved on and started a consulting business at home. I began writing and giving seminars and talks on soft-skill topics related to my graduate degree in Organizational Management. This was not satisfying. I often wrote business and marketing plans for small business owners while longing to write a self-help or how-to book. As a frustrated writer, authoring my personal stories when I could, I taught part-time at the university and began plans to research a business book for consulting.

Did you allow "breathing room" with your stories?

Yes. I was open from the beginning. I chose the high road and did not expound to the point that my scenes would become too graphic. My goal has always been to motivate others, not to rant. I'm intuitive and a good judge of people, so I searched for the truth for my readers. I determined I'd go beyond my baby boomer generation, my niche market, to find my secondary and primary audiences. Breathing room creates flexibility.

The readers make up their own minds. They read my stories, see what I have done and how I have evolved, and draw their own conclusions. After working diligently to write a compelling narrative and enticing dialogue, I put it out there, telling my story and no one else's.

Do your readers have a "reason to care" when they turn the page?

Yes, they do. My chapters are filled with information, and solutions as well. In some way, my story becomes their story, endearing them to me through my words and the stories' resolutions. I present them with conflicts and obstacles. They relate by personally identifying with me, a family member, a friend, or a neighbor by seeing what happened to me and how I survived.

My goal was to pique their empathy, to show the steps to make a delightful story out of trauma. I also wanted to show the red flags I ignored in my life and give them the facts.

Stories on critical, timely topics such as alcohol recovery, love addiction, domestic violence, and post-traumatic stress required leaving my ego behind. My critique group members ensured that happened by reading my pages with a critical eye.

Do you read other material while you're drafting a book?

Yes. I must read to be able to write. Initially, I read only memoirs, self-help, and how-to books. Today I occasionally read fiction if I know it is based on actual events. The book must focus on human rights. Spiritual books also help enhance my soul when I write.

I take God with me when I write, to stay peaceful as I rummage through my memory for the story. I usually read at least two books at once. I choose to buy books from local authors, first from the women in my writers' group, or our meeting speakers. Eventually, I draft a book review for them, despite the time and effort it takes, because it is important.

Has your education helped your writing?

Yes, but not directly. When I embarked on graduate school, I focused on another business degree and a 180-page feasibility study to decide my entrepreneurial future. My thesis demanded a tremendous amount of work with much statistical information. Although I did not publish my thesis, I proved that my plan to open a women's clothing business in the mid-1980s in Scottsdale was not possible. If I had published my thesis, it would have been my first book, but not my favorite book.

I might have launched a new career with a thesis on a publication-worthy topic. Instead, God's plan guided me to go a different direction with my writing and create personal stories. I wrote whenever possible, even with no goal of a book, recalling memories of what was said and done. Through my writing, I accepted the lessons learned.

I wrote about what I loved with passion, to inspire and motivate others, help them, and educate them. I had to write if I was going to survive. My business experience became valuable when I began my publishing company and started marketing my books. The extensive sales and marketing experience I'd gained in business gave me an advantage in many areas.

What was the myth, the secret about your life, you knew you had changed?

Many people considered me a one-dimensional, business-oriented person. After being assaulted and losing my sister to lung cancer, I vowed not to give up my dream to draft my personal stories. I set my first writing goal: to help others with their grief journey. I thought I might choose to write a memoir, but it chose me.

With my graduate degree in hand, I taught part-time at Arizona State University and the Maricopa County Community College District. I wrote curriculum for the university to supplement my income and built a small training business from home. I wrote what I thought would be my first book, *Soft Skills for Employee Training*. That stopped when my sister became ill.

While attending a few writing classes at Phoenix College, I authored stories about my relationship with my youngest sister and addressed how siblings play a critical role in our lives.

The only way to draft that book was to put all my feelings down on paper, to select words that described her and how I felt about her and our relationship at the time. Selecting this part of my life changed me forever. I faced my loss and grief head-on. I felt compelled to tell our story. I had never felt so much pain before the agony of her loss. Writing was my answer.

Will you write the marketing book at another time?

Someday I may go back to business writing. Right now, telling my stories is my passion. Writing *Gifts of Sisterhood: Journey from Grief to Gratitude* was a very painful but necessary task during an integral part of my life. Yet, by telling the story of our relationship and how her humility and grace showed me how to face life, I could write my next two memoirs. Suffering gave the story energy and meaning.

With her death, I shifted from writing business articles to writing memoirs and polishing my speeches for Toastmasters International. Making these moves, I could tell the truth in my memoirs on love addiction and recovery. Each piece of this puzzle, each part of the path to writing this self-help book, gave me time to heal. The gap in the schedule and sequence between the first book and the last two served a purpose. You are ready to finish a book only when the book is ready. It already exists inside of you.

A lifelog scribbler and avid notetaker, I also served as a reporter for my community college newspaper in the 1970s in Glen Ellyn, Illinois. These activities set the tone for the writing life I have and need today. During those years, I wrote for the sheer pleasure of it, as a hobby. That changed when I met my current husband, Earl. He encouraged me to write what I wanted and not hold back.

I had heard that repeatedly in writing seminars. To hear it from my husband provoked a day of reckoning, a decisive moment. He loved to read. Like me, he loved to read biographies and memoirs. He encouraged me all the way to share my emotional beats, those gut-wrenching stories deep in my soul. Like me, he loves facts, conflicts, obstacles, and solutions. We are on track together, reading and drafting our stories—a peaceful environment for both of us.

What motivated you to come back to your writing?

I could not stifle the urge inside of me anymore. My first book was "a savior." Still, I knew there was more for me to write. I gave a lot to others over that five-year period, between 2005 and 2010. I founded my women writers club, the Scottsdale Society of Women Writers. My husband and I started our publishing company, Brooks Goldmann Publishing, LLC. I wore a business hat ahead of a writer's hat, writing sporadically without any purpose.

When my husband slowed down, played less golf, and took my advice to start writing his first memoir, I knew we were a writing team. I picked up my writing pace and committed to my last two memoirs and this book you hold in your hand

I challenged myself to draft the books I always wanted to write. I took the advice I gave to members of my writing group: don't stop. We revamped our company to engage more freelancers. We freed up more time to make writing our priority. We became utterly obsessed with writing and researching, visualizing scenes, hearing dialogue, and setting goals.

I felt ready for an exhilarating stint of writing every day. Those days did not disappoint me. My husband wrote diligently too.

Where do you go when you write?

I go to my heart and soul. It's always been in me to express myself. I love pen and paper and am eager for more conversation.

Taking my stories from my subconscious to my heart and soul, then to the paper or laptop, gives me time to collaborate with them.

I love to tell stories, to express myself emotionally. I come from a family of storytellers. I make people laugh and have a good sense of humor. I'm not surprised when people laugh at what I say. Writing saved my life more than once. In my books, I make sense of my life by telling my stories and shifting from internal to external expression.

To heal my heart, I pursued these key areas with my writing:

- Creating dialogues.
- Unraveling narratives.
- Using my imagination.
- Telling my truth.
- Showing my authenticity.
- Baring my honest emotions, my soul.

This starting point is critical to my sanity. By attending workshops and conferences, both locally and nationally, I read, imagine, and write words that have power for me. I use those words wisely. A daily journal works for me since I like to write things down. I clear my thoughts, write my truth, and let my imagination run wild.

Writing is a compulsion. I crave it. I feel starved for writing if I don't get my chance to write and create an idea. I only write about my thoughts and feelings, commenting only on my experiences. I do not make assumptions about others. No matter how certain I am about my life, I cannot emphatically know what motivates others. Even when my thoughts flow like a river, I must decipher the truth I know for sure.

Each piece of my writing becomes a new adventure, prompted by what I am reading, have read, or my current or past experiences. I am obsessed with words. They are my escape. It's rare for me to say no to writing. Like many of the creatives in my family, I pride myself on contributing my part to the creative world. I am the only writer, except for my husband. There are artists, singers, and crafty types, but I stand alone with my talents, which is a gift I appreciate.

I credit my accomplishments to many authors of spiritual and recovery books. One of my favorites, Dr. Wayne Dyer, influenced me for many years. I read a lot of his books. Harvey Mackay, a prolific writer of business books, inspired and motivated me. I still read his column online.

Most recently, I read Maria Shriver's online content for my source for spiritual thought. I have read several of her books too. She is light, intuitive, intelligent, forgiving, and loving. Her purpose has taken her to many incredible places, even beyond her Kennedy lineage. I look forward to her blog on Sunday mornings.

I create time and space to write in my home office, the library, or a coffee shop, and do it with or without a plan. As an adept wordsmith, I can manage the alone time it takes to write. I am not lonely. My words fill a void as I describe scenes vividly.

What is your advice to new memoir writers?

Everybody can write something. Most don't get around to it. Only a few try it or do it. Be proud, as I am, when you author your book. It is quite an accomplishment.

Keep in mind:
- Stay young-hearted and full of fresh ideas.
- Don't stop writing.
- Remember, it's a way to create energy, to get to know yourself.
- Be grateful for positive influences.

The book *Little Women* by Louisa May Alcott influenced me the most in my youth. I am grateful for her book about the wonderful March sisters Jo, Beth, Amy, and Meg. I followed their loves, lives, and tribulations. Jo was my favorite. The book is based on the true-life story of the author and her three sisters. I had three sisters too.

20. Networking for Authors

> *Your network is your net worth!*
> — Porter Gale, internationally renowned public speaker

Making an impression

Do you hate the idea of networking? Do you consider yourself a shy author? Does networking feel unnatural to you? Do you shun the idea because it is too aggressive for you?

If you answered yes to one or more of these questions, you're like most writers who value their time to write more than book promotion. Networking is more difficult for writers who are alone most of the day. You must step out of the vacuum.

Even if an authors' "networking night" is forced on you at some point, you must attempt to learn how to sell books face-to-face:

- Carefully develop your voice.
- Courageously pursue your efforts to promote.
- Know you're not alone.
- Get into the writer's life.

Creating first impressions

Your appearance, language, and attitude are critical to your image. If, as an author, you fail to take any of these seriously, your books will not sell.

Your reputation will suffer in more ways than you can imagine if you do not:
- Dress well when speaking online, on a podcast, or on a Zoom call.
- Take time to build your book business.
- Demonstrate you are a respected author in your genre and in your communities.
- Learn to be comfortable with your newfound title.

Competition abounds, and that makes the world go around. Connecting one-on-one in a group is the best form of networking. Stay focused and be prepared.

Speaking allows you to express your ideas:
- Prepare in advance what you plan to say and do.
- Check out the event, conference, or speaking engagement early.
- Learn as much as you can about the experience you are about to have with them.
- Get to know the organizer and the key people in the audience.
- Believe in yourself and what you are doing.
- Have fun and enjoy the ride.

Remember, the networking game is necessary in a writer's life. Prove yourself useful to the other writers and authors you associate with. You will do well and be a happy author.

Joining professional organizations

Professional organizations outside of your writers' group serve as a major source for networking. They should be groups associated with one of your book's topics. Join or affiliate with them. In the case of domestic violence, the topic of my second book, I have been involved for some time with the Arizona Center to End Sexual and Domestic Violence. I've made connections as an adjunct faculty member at Arizona State University, who has taught for more than twenty years. The contacts I made through church and volunteering in the world of recovery relate to my third book. These meaningful relationships helped me escape my comfort zone, writing in isolation. I contact people and organizations from my present and my past and any other group I find interesting, whether a civic or religious group, school, or business. I increase my visibility.

Try this approach:
- Choose organizations well, as you did for the main theme of your book.
- Give them much thought, so they will be more attracted to you, and you them.
- Gently ask to speak to their group.
- Consider joining Toastmasters.
- Read books on public speaking.
- Be willing to share your stories, even if they are very personal.

Writing groups

Network with your writing group colleagues. Be active in a writing group, a critique group, a book club, or any educational opportunity for writers.

Go further and do the following:
- Be an officer, a leader, or even the founder of a writing group.
- Volunteer as the membership chairperson.
- Attend an outside writers' event and report back to the group.
- Mentor an aspiring writer in the group.
- Organize an outside event for your writing group.
- Cross-brand your books with a writer friend by posting information on each other's websites

These actions are a sure-fire way to expand your audience by promoting your books and yourself as a reputable author. Brand yourself further with a blog, newsletter, or podcast. These offerings are paramount to your success with social media. These efforts create cross-branding opportunities with other authors of a similar genre. Instagram highlights visual stories, while Facebook offers an author community. Goodreads is like book heaven for reviews and recommendations, while LinkedIn provides a professional approach to your "new" business writing and selling books.

Use podcasts, YouTube videos, online interviews, and guest blogger invitations too. Remember, your purpose is to establish yourself and get to know your people, your community. You'll succeed when you do this process correctly. When planning your strategy, start locally, move to metro, then to state levels. Go after the national and international arenas last. Somebody must do it. Why not you? See yourself as the expert.

I suggest the following:

- Always tell your writing colleagues how to stay in touch with you.
- Give them your social media information and your professional website link.
- Make this contact effort work for you and your book.
- Volunteer at a conference or book festival to raise your visibility.

Plan to actively network on a weekly basis. Be authentic with your efforts to give back and you will receive what you need.

Meet with others one-on-one as well. The writer reaps the benefits of networking by sharing resources and being the first to give back. Be professional, pique others' interest, and be nonthreatening to spike sales. You never know where you'll unearth the best information. Never think you are above anybody in a writing group.

The general media, newspapers, TV stations, and talk radio shows can be your friends. Please try to know these professionals, and so endear them to you by sending them quality media releases and news information. They need you to fill in the space by sending them information that answers questions about you and your book. You can find press release templates online. Just remember the who, what, when, where, why, and how of the story.

Media reps are terribly busy people, so contact them and you can help by making their work easier. Media professionals are usually willing to publicize your book when you collaborate with them. Face your fears and send out press releases to appropriate contacts.

Writing events

Participating in writing events at various locations, including bookstores, libraries, and conferences, is critical to your success. If only one person attends your event or talk and buys your book, you have succeeded. You only have one chance with your book presentation. You will never know who that special person is if you are not open to embracing the writer's life.

You will make yourself known through creative networking when you:

- Attend conferences for writing, publishing, or marketing books.
- Participate in workshops with your peers, other authors, or publishers.
- Glean writing information from everywhere that works for you.
- Get to know the competition and learn from them.
- Always wear your writing hat.
- Seek all things writing related. Participate in writing classes.
- Use information from books on writing.
- Send a handwritten thank-you note to the author you heard speak.
- Draft a review for the book you purchased to let them know what you write.

You receive what you give in this writing life. "Do onto others" applies. Read and review books in your genre, especially those that pop up next to yours on a bookshelf or online search.

It takes a lot of effort and willingness to try new things in this competitive industry.

Stay in the herd by:
- Responding immediately when anyone in the writing world seeks you out.
- Finding a way to answer their questions promptly.
- Asking how they found you. Was it a personal referral or by happenstance?
- Researching to find out what type of networking is helpful to you.
- Communicating more through your community's websites or blogs.

Selling books

Selling books is not only about talking to family and friends or using email and personal announcements. Selling books online, and in person by preparing and making eye contact, can be a solid income stream. You will reach a larger audience. To sell books, remember people love to read books. You are offering them a great service, but you must be willing to:
- Meet your readers face-to-face or online and tell them about your stories.
- Thank your community for doing what it takes to share your benefits with others.
- Seek out people on social media and other digital options.
- Stay consistent, follow up, and stay focused, despite the slightest rejection.

Most importantly, basic networking means being prepared. Bring a business card or bookmark to hand out at a writing conference, a monthly writers' meeting, an author's book event, or wherever you deem appropriate. These scenarios require you to dress well, talk to others, listen, and ask questions, all while being friendly and approachable. Most importantly, make eye contact when selling in person to validate you are the author of a noteworthy work.

Adding to your exposure

Reaching a higher level as a networker in the world of writing and publishing requires you to listen more than you talk. This is not always easy at an in-person networking opportunity or on social media. Most authors tend to be overzealous at such events. Adhere to the following to help you once you have established a win-win relationship:

- Don't be afraid to reach out and show interest.
- Be genuine and authentic.
- Ask your target audiences to sign up for your email newsletter or blog.
- Suggest they follow your author page online.
- Direct your new contacts or potential readers to visit your author's website.
- Develop your list of contacts and readers from those you meet.
- View this exposure as a critical building block for your community.
- Budget funds to attend a local, state, or national writers' conference.

These efforts are the key to your success, especially when you follow up and do what you said you would do. These contacts help you transition into the writing world, even if you feel vulnerable. Your well-planned actions may land you a writing coach to hold you accountable or an editor to polish your work. By networking with intention, you can work successfully with others in this new life, giving and receiving.

Other ways to network:

- Use social media including Facebook, Twitter, and Instagram.
- Consider searching YouTube and TikTok for newer books to read.
- Work to avoid offending anyone by being too much of a hard sell.

- Avoid pressuring others to do anything for you or your book.
- Politely ask them to pass your name or the name of your book on to someone else.
- Word-of-mouth marketing is still the best form of networking.
- Understand it is an opportunity to move your positive image forward.

Social media provides a forum to elaborate on why you chose this life while, at the same time, informing your blog or website readers why they should pick up your book. Pay attention and address their responses to catapult your success.

Readings and book signings

Do not forget bookstores, online forums, in-person conversations and events, and libraries. You meet people at those venues whose lives are books. You are now in that circle.

For support, get to know librarians, bookstore owners, and book lovers online:
- Alert all the local bookstores in your state.
- Connect with all the libraries in your current metro area.
- Start local with promotion.
- Follow that up in your hometown, wherever you live.
- Develop your website and expand nationally and internationally.
- Explain well what you are doing now with your writing or newest book.
- Seek out opportunities at book fairs and literary festivals.
- Attend a writing retreat or conference in another area to meet new people.

I visited my hometown and participated in events for all three of my memoirs. Some book signings were done in coffee shops, while others were at the local library. I sought media coverage, just as I did in the state where I live. I traveled thousands of miles to speak about my books. I am happy I did not miss the chance to go back to my roots, and you shouldn't either.

Becoming authentic

Key to networking success: make yourself comfortable going solo by being authentic and trustworthy. Being likeable on social media and in person is essential, and you don't have to try so hard you lose peace and calm. No need to panic.

Consider working with some of these philosophies:
- Be careful talking about your personal life unless it relates to your memoir.
- Never complain about anything relating to you or your book.
- Remain the consummate professional.
- Distance yourself from those trying to trap you with a question on social media.
- Keep politics out of your presentations unless it relates to your book.
- Network and sell in person and online or hire a publicity person.

These above ideas backfire if you remain distant from others. On the other hand, check yourself to ensure you are not too aggressive with "buy my book."

Authors are naturally casual by nature. They know they cannot please everyone every time. If the event requires giving away a book, do it. If it requires you be subtle with your promotion, do it. Take time to evaluate every networking situation and be creative with your improvements.

Asking for reviews

Asking for reviews of your book is a great tool. It adds to your credibility and generates sales when you present online or speak to a group. I often give a book away in exchange for a review on Amazon or Goodreads. You must constantly expose the masses to your books.

My books create positive reviews because they are valuable to the reader, so I ask for feedback. The readers feel grateful. These reviews are contagious and often ignite the sale of another one of my other books. This is due to the overlapping themes and the "bundle" style of branding them as a continuation of the first or second book. I believe in my books, and you can believe in yours.

Do not be afraid to "ask for the order" with a review. Most people are happy to accommodate you. A sincere and quality review is gold. Obtaining this support needs to be part of your "I need to spend money to earn more money" philosophy. Give books away, buy an ad, or do a "sale" day. Book sales will increase because of your generosity.

Some of the most successful authors I know regularly give away their books. I support that philosophy. It raises the bar when it is offered as a gift to help someone, illuminating my work. It removes any stigma attached to the topics when used to help others.

Building long-term relationships

Networking is a long-term relationship in the making. Randomly handing out business cards at an event is in the past. You truly begin to know the people you want to sell to now or with a repeat sale. The goal is to build your network for the long term and to take time with these contacts. The process for authors is quite different from the traditional style of business networking. A "little schmoozing" goes a long way. You and your contacts are both busy. Respect them to earn their respect.

Consider the following:
- Give something of value to win them over, such as an innovative marketing idea.
- Talk about your book and yourself after you listen first.
- Start close to home. Then move to national exposure.
- Build your network and your community.

Those who know you or are familiar with you are your first line of sight: friends and family, colleagues and former business associates, neighbors, and personal connections. Make a list of those people who fall into one or several of these categories. Many of the people you've met along your life's path will be the most interested in hearing from you and about your success.

21. Age, a Gift to My Writing

> *Aging is not "lost youth" but a new stage*
> *of opportunity and strength.*
>
> — Betty Friedan, American feminist writer and activist

Too often, we're amazed by writers who author books late in life. But why should we be surprised? Margaret Atwood wrote at age eighty-two. Toni Morrison published at eighty-four. Agatha Christie wrote until the end of her life at eighty-four. *In Changing Minds,* by Richard Roberts, he says seniors average 20,000 words in their vocabulary. College students average about 16,000 words. Other research studies confirm this.

Something about a late bloomer inspires us. For us creative types, hope is all we need to start. Laura Ingalls Wilder, who authored *Little House in the Woods,* is one of my favorite examples because her work went on to become *Little House on the Prairie,* a TV success story starring Melissa Gilbert. The best part for me? Meeting Gilbert several years ago at her book signing tour stop here in Phoenix. She spoke on her memoir, *Prairie Tale.* I read her book and thoroughly enjoyed it.

If we keep reading, journaling, and writing, we can carry on limitlessly into our sixties, seventies, eighties, and beyond. The Yale Center for Research on Aging has learned when seniors read at least thirty minutes a day, they live on average two to four years longer than their peers. Reading, writing, and learning extend our lives by using our brains cognitively and from the sheer joy of writing and telling our stories. Being productive and positive at all stages of life advances our hope for literary or other creative success.

Some of us are late bloomers. We take writing classes and attend conferences for writers, some for the first time as seniors. While others desire a partner or ghostwriter to help reach the goal of publication. We know how to stay optimistic and hopeful and to make a commitment to publishing our memoirs. By living our dreams, we succeed in the end.

I began in my fifties. The challenges of my earlier sales career pushed me to be the best. I see now how terribly competitive those days were. I was obsessed with winning, recognition, and earning awards. Those accolades weren't enough. Something was missing.

My semi-retirement allowed me to begin to write beyond my journals. When I turned away from a sales career after thirty-plus years and pursued my creative side, I felt younger. The busier I became, the less I thought about my age. Writing my memoirs was not the goal of my youth, but certainly captured the focus of my adult life.

Authoring my stories with ease and patience as I aged gracefully helped me glean insight and wisdom about life—mine and others'. It saved me from stress and frustration and offered the opportunity to live my best life in good health. Today, I will author my stories at a time when I am comfortable in my own skin.

My age and experience enrich my words and stories in each of my three memoirs. I've grown as a writer. I want success for myself and my readers too. Every day, I seek to create something with my writing.

I came closer to more innovative ideas because I experienced:
- Forgiveness in my heart.
- A sweeping view of the beauty of life.
- Gratitude for all my life stories.
- Acceptance of the stories' limitations.

Living life well is invaluable to the senior writer's overall happiness. As a woman of a certain age, I appreciate being a storyteller while remembering long-forgotten events. Today, my best creativity surfaces when I have the courage to just write, unconcerned with what others think. That is the beauty of aging graciously with tolerance. By taking emotional risks with my innovation, my experiences help others. I push myself a little further every day and work on my projects to honor the parts of me worth sharing. Staying healthy by eating well gives me energy to read and write. Being physically active with tennis, walking, and yoga adds to the vitality senior life requires.

When I walked through the door of a writing career, the opportunities were limitless. I believed if I had a writing project and stayed engaged, it would progress well and eventually come to fruition. Time was on my side with my flexible work-at-home schedule. I've done this now since the year 2000.

I easily worked the pandemic stay-at-home lifestyle into my schedule. I nurtured each new chapter with the belief that hours of writing and critiquing would keep my mind sharp. It took time for me to grow with each memoir. My writing had to age with my increased knowledge.

Since my stories were so personal, I worked diligently with the chapter topics and readied myself to peel the onion and share them. For me—and countless other seniors, including my husband—writing is one of the most stimulating and accessible projects we can try. You only need a journal or notepad and a pen to start, and you can write in coffee shops, at home, in the park, or at the library. No large expense needed to begin.

Writing showed my husband and me there were no limits to what we could do and carry out, including learning how to self-publish and market our own work. From our childhood stories to our coming-of-age stories, we captured our thoughts. We made space for each other to write and dedicated our second bedroom as a home office. We allowed quiet time. I wrote in the "makeshift office," and he wrote at the dining room table.

Expressing our creativity most mornings stimulates our intellect and supports our longevity. My husband and I converse, share, and help each other find words and ideas. We proofread each other's work and give positive constructive criticism. We respect each other's voices, honor our uniqueness, and achieve a comfort level with our past lives.

My first three memoirs overlap. My stories cross paths yet differ. They cover various aspects of my life at contrasting times. My generation, the baby boomers, exemplifies getting into a little trouble, desiring freedom, and creating mischief. My husband and I no longer choose trouble with strong consequences, those we can't get out of quickly. We stir up feelings with our writing instead by sharing our generational emotional voice with our memoirs and personal essays.

Each of my memoirs helps the reader by creating emotional connectedness to my deep topics.

My memoirs have guided me for the following reasons:

- Writing preserves memories.
- Keeping a journal, while writing, confirms commitment.
- Writing projects and deadlines add structure to retirement life.
- Journaling and writing free our stories for our legacy.
- Writing opens a gateway to the past for many generations.
- Memoirs written later in life instill appreciation for a long life.

My memoirs, and those of my husband, were written with heart-wrenching honesty. They were cathartic at the time of their writing and changed us as writers and as a couple. We write better today and are freer in our communication than when we first met twenty years ago. I started writing my first book at that time. We grew with our love of reading and writing, while honoring our memoirs. They are a gift from God to us and our readers.

We know life is short. We don't bristle with receiving criticism and understand:

- The desire in our souls to be authentic.
- Our trust, with God's grace, our memories will be appreciated.
- Not to judge each other's writing. We emulate a face of understanding.
- The eagerness in our hearts to learn more through one another.

I did not initially dwell on the past. I used it as my strength. I learned lessons and found solutions. Now, later in life, I am receptive to gleaning more about people for my stories. The struggles I endured in my young adult life gave me courage and insight. Each year brings meaning to many things but not the intention to slow down. I feel younger.

Attending my fiftieth high school class reunion in 2018 felt bittersweet. Seeing how long-time friends changed with age—not recognizing some, knowing others immediately—was all part of the fun. I felt grateful to be there. Being present without expectation felt freeing and opened up more stories.

I was sure conversations would revolve around band trips to Canada or cheerleading and sports in the late 1960s. Instead, we spent time with those we least expected. New friendships were born. The usual cheerleading picture did not happen. It wasn't as important this time. The group picture was organized the way it should be. We all posed together with big smiles on that beautiful Michigan summer night. My mantra was "enjoy the moment," for these are the best of times for all of us.

At this reunion, an old friend introduced me to his new wife. He called me a cheerleader extraordinaire. It amused me since I'd lived a successful and busy life beyond 1968, including my current—third, and most rewarding—career. Writing my memoirs tells the real story. We never really left high school. Often, those years form the barometer for our values and desires in life and create prompts for senior writers. During those crucial years, we paved habits, interests, and relationships while setting ourselves up for decades to come.

A few years earlier, I held two book signings in my hometown featuring my third memoir, one at a coffee shop and one at the local library. Fewer classmates attended this time. partially because I had been there five years earlier. And, of course, life itself.

Mostly, community residents attended. I had not known them since I had left for college fifty years earlier. Those who did attend encouraged me to keep writing and share my stories. Others said they had writing goals themselves. Write, write, and rewrite defined the philosophy of the night.

Encouraging my Korean War-era husband to keep writing and visualize another book has helped his mental health. This process makes him happy. He enjoys the quiet of reading and becoming absorbed in his writing. He did not retire mentally after leaving his life-long career. His writing brings back fond memories for him. We have similar goals: leave a legacy, keep active, and add to our positive mental health. We relearned how to create, and how to take our manuscripts to fruition. We enrich our life together as we go along by reading and appreciating the arts and attending plays or movies in the area.

Like me, he had the desire to write from an early age. He started at age seventy-eight, gifting his readers with a lot of stories. Some make the reader cry, some encourage a ready smile, and some give pause.

My personal, creative writing started around age fifty, after my years of business and academic writing. We know we can't just write for ourselves. We must give to our writing community by participating in events to support our fellow authors.

The illusion of agelessness supplies fodder for both of us to produce our best work. I poke fun at myself with my writings, and he does too. This attitude makes it joyous and stress-free. We don't distract ourselves and are prepared and ready if life issues take up some of our time. We share our writing life completely.

My husband has authored more stories than I have about childhood, high school, and college. Most of my memoirs start with high school, then quickly move on to how the decisions I made at that early age and in my young adulthood affected my life going forward. Our memoirs inspire the reader to seek the solutions gleaned from life experiences.

I approach my writing and teaching memoir writing as follows:

- Finding empathy for those who are stuck in the past.
- Remembering how far we have come by finding joy in the journey.
- Being sensitive to my character.

- Being open to learning more about my craft.
- Letting go of issues that control me.

Though I left my hometown for college more than fifty years ago, my husband and I return every other summer to visit. Even though the pandemic adjusted that schedule, it did not alter our need to write and reconnect with our histories. That desire has not changed for me and my hometown of St. Ignace, or for my husband and Tillamook, Oregon.

My husband and I own our regrets. We all have them. We do it for our friends, family, followers, readers, and ourselves. This opportunity comes with age.

In doing so, we learn who we are. Our books reflect these desires by bringing authenticity to our writing. Our partnership helps both of us. Self-acceptance is our goal. We know we have much to offer and don't judge ourselves. We are better at our game after all these years.

I experience no sadness in aging. The mid-seventies today are the mid-sixties of a decade ago. I've lived thirty-plus years longer than my younger sister who died of lung cancer at age forty-four. This reality was brought home to me when I wrote my first book about her. She remains with me in spirit. I have had a similar experience of gratitude with my other memories too.

I take emotional risks with my writing by telling my readers about the dysfunction in my past life and how I turned it around. It's never too late to repair the stories we've learned from on our journey. Finding empathy for other women who need to tell their stories allows me to reach out to them on related topics.

Gifts of Sisterhood, initially published in 2005, remains ageless. Despite our losses, the beauty of a memoir lives forever.

My experience with my readers and this book is incredible. It is my pleasure to share my youngest sister's story with those who loved her and knew her and others who want to know her. In some ways, it lives as our coming-of-age story. The book took on a life of its own, becoming a featured story in the *Breadthways Newsletter* for the Arizona Lung Association, which launched the core of my *Stop Smoking Sister* campaign.

A side benefit of writing memoir is to take it to another level by:

- Understanding the past to create a new reality.
- Seeking the spiritual side of life to make sense of it all.

Three Husbands and a Thousand Boyfriends was published in 2016 with stories about surviving domestic violence, an assault, and love addiction. My experience had resulted in two trials, civil and criminal. My advice is to give yourself a break from internal judgment, as I did. Don't give up on anything. Write about it all.

Domestic violence crosses all age groups, education levels, ethnicities, and backgrounds. By expressing myself genuinely and telling what happened, and by feeling whole and sharing what happened to me during those violent acts, I came out the other side with forgiveness and self-acceptance. This book came to fruition with this insight, the wisdom of age, and the knowledge we can all start fresh again.

I visited my hometown community to do a book signing event for *Sick as My Secrets* at the local library. I shared my growth with friends and family. With a heartfelt voice, I felt proud of how far I had traveled.

With this latest memoir, I moved forward to another productive phase of my life by openly sharing more than forty years of recovery from alcoholism. This disclosure is my finest work. I can help many with my story. When asked to talk about my recovery story, I do not hesitate. I focus on my positive energy.

With this memoir, I moved forward to find my inner writer, who had been resting for a while. When my husband and I returned from vacation, we launched my book in our local Scottsdale community. We showed the audience of friends how writing is creative work, despite the battles we share.

By using my God-given writing talent, a whole new world and third career opened up to me. I felt my feelings about age, imagination, health, time, and space. Appreciating my writing skills and honoring my creativity as a published author showed up in my stories. My wisdom and insight about my writer's life over the past twenty years and my ability and knowledge as a workshop presenter are paramount to my legacy as a writer.

No age barrier exists for me or you. My authentic talks to the community, law enforcement, students, church groups, and others are well received. I will never stifle sharing what I feel strongly about in relation to events that touched my life. Healing through grief, loss, and trauma has motivated me to inspire others of any age to value their diverse situations and to put their stories on paper. I urge them to drop any judgment they have about their feelings or themselves and work for enlightenment and hope. To be okay with a little anxiety.

My attitude is to:

- Seek patience in finding yourself with each version of your manuscript.
- Be eager to connect with your past to encourage and inspire others.

By concentrating on reading, writing, teaching, and mentoring other men and women, we contribute to our society in creative ways. These actions allow us to be the person we always knew we could be. To give back in this way has many rewards, humility being one. It offers me an opportunity to share my story through writing and speaking. Once I have looked back and accepted it, my goal is to fire on all cylinders and look forward.

Persistence is a critical factor in achieving anything. I do not give up. I regroup and redefine my book business and writing projects each year. Being adaptable in my writing life over the past twenty years has allowed me to help other writers. My generation is not selfless. We dispel that myth with our creativity. By learning to share the wisdom of our experiences in our tales, we become a gift to others.

I learn so much when I teach my Write the Memoir You're Afraid to Write workshop. Beginning with the writing process and ending with my creativity, my written words and voice embody a spiritual experience. Passing on to the audience the knowledge I've gained over many years means helping each writer see their story as a tool to aid the reader. It reinforces the need to live purposefully as we commit to a strong project.

Each year I teach, I improve my writing. Age is the greatest gift to my work, in all areas. It humbles me. Makes me proud. Gives me the courage to share freely what I know. I see things more clearly and act accordingly, and don't talk myself out of any opportunity.

Coming from a generation of idealism, believing in the impossible lives in my soul. These shared beliefs breathe in the hearts of the women in my writers' group, Scottsdale Society of Women Writers. Many of the members have taken control of their writing life in their unique way.

We write about something we know, something we care about, and:

- We give back by supporting one another.
- We encourage one another.
- We build our group together as a safe place for women to pursue their writing,
- We find immense pride in being part of this collective group.

My generation is often stereotyped as self-indulgent. Still, I am proud to be a member. By joining my peers who write freely, we redefine our lives and age gracefully. We have a lot to share about the changes in older adulthood. A new wave of writing creatively emerges and allows our activism to appear.

Many baby boomer women today are youthful and optimistic. We have lofty expectations of ourselves, express our voices vividly, and look to our creative and spiritual lives to sustain us. We hold on to our belief that we are stronger today, and we ache to tell our stories and let them be a part of us. We no longer think life revolves around us. We choose to make things happen through our stories. We did not trust anyone over thirty "back in the day." We now trust each other for support of our creative efforts.

We realize we can't afford to lie down. We have things to create, words to write, and voices to share. Being comfortable at this age as a writer means being willing to share our lives in memoirs and articles and send them out for publication. Not to be afraid to be heard.

I offer my best to you in this book. I continue to write and share with excitement. Through the struggle, we persevere and remain strong in the face of adversity. We've proven this. Writing memoirs is all about having grace for our family, friends, and readers. As we go toward the truth, we push ourselves to release stress and be healthy with our creativity.

If there is pent-up anger, angst, or sadness in our words, we will ourselves to do our best work by:

- Staying energized and excited about this new chapter in our lives.
- Writing from a specific juncture where we developed with age.
- Affirm, "I dare to do this writing work."
- Work on a project that reflects us.

The fight is worth it, even if we never win an award. We create our own opportunities as truth tellers. We learn about ourselves and our world. The beauty of our work is age free.

We usually mature gracefully and accept the cycle of life. What is important to us in this mode is to leave a mark from a place of beauty. To live our lives; give back; connect with people; strengthen our minds, bodies, and souls; and love ourselves. We are jewels in the rough in society until we free ourselves with writing and share our innermost secrets and stories. As we age, we are eager to learn more about things we did not have time to pursue earlier in life, and that is the beauty of writing.

APPENDIX 1

Author Platform

The author platform is comparable to the listenership of a specific radio station or the viewership of a particular television program.
— Shawna Morey, former literary agent at Folio

Once you have written your memoir and it is in the editing process, or even earlier, write your "author platform." It will give you visibility in the world of books, influence others to read your work, and help you reach more of a fringe audience than with random promotions. Your goal is to be ready to market yourself through your skills, your background, your ability, and all the information you share on social media.

The author platform includes the avenues you use to speak to your readers in today's digital world. Podcasts, videos, and social media outlets augment traditional public speaking opportunities. For all of this, you need to ask yourself, "Who will be listening, and who do I need to listen to?"

What to include in your author platform.

Your brand proves your credibility statement. It is your key to selling books, because your brand represents who you are, your experiences, and who you can reach through your personal marketing.

The author platform must include the following:
- Your impressive, professional website/blog.
- A mailing list worth talking about to an agent or media outlet.
- Any and all articles or blogs you have written for others in the past year.
- Other guest posts on successful websites or blogs related to your theme.
- A history of strong book sales.
- Endorsements from influential people you know.
- Any and all public speaking appearances.
- A positive and productive "giving back" social media presence.
- Memberships in credible writing groups and related organizations.
- Ongoing media appearances and interviews in print, radio, TV, and online.

The goal of the author platform is to create a unique voice.

The author platform is critical in the promotion of memoir and nonfiction books, especially when self-published. When you develop your plan, remember your main message requires you create a unique brand with an authentic voice. Differentiation is key in marketing. You want it to work for you. Build relationships by serving up a consistent message, pulling people to you. While there are more than one hundred social media outlets, you need only work four to six consistently to drive your marketing.

The following activities are paramount to your author platform success:
- Develop a media branding kit with a tagline, your colors, photos, and logo.
- Consider an online book tour, similar to your face-to-face tour.
- To further connect, research bookstores in your immediate area and beyond.
- Update your website to stay current.
- Build marketing "buzz" with an email list, blog posts, and social media postings.
- Strive to keep a consistent message about you and your "brand."

The core ideas and principles of your author platform.

You must think of your author platform as a gift to your readers, the media, and anyone else interested in your writing life. It displays what you give to the world, authentically and positively.

You don't have to do this alone. Many opportunities exist to engage a mentor, coach, or partner on your journey. Remember, the platform is what you want for your brand now, not based on your past laurels, except to establish credibility.

Authors often learn from their heroes' success stories and even emulate them and work with their ideas. We have all learned from role models including our parents, teachers, friends, and colleagues. Your responsibility lies in working to become your best self to attain success in the competitive world of books.

My recommendations are:
- Start locally and small. Then move to a second tier and, as you learn, even further.
- Write out your author platform plan and be flexible.
- Brand yourself as a likeable and endearing character for your readers.

- Quantify your author platform with regard to your book's budget.
- Take advantage of providing something people want.
- Market and promote easily and steadily, not as a hard sell.
- Always have a goal for the event, the promotion, or your presence.
- Market yourself first by showing the benefits of buying your book and supporting you.

How do I find my "niche" in this maze of branding?

By keeping in mind your memoir theme and threads, and what you represent to the reading audiences, you will stay visible in this busy business of selling books. The author platform is not about your credentials. It's about what you are doing now to rise above the fray of publishing and promotion. It's about using the most generic form of communication that works for you, whether emails, text messages, podcasts, or any of the many offerings available. You choose what form of communication will best represent you, your brand, and your book.

Consider these questions as you do a rough draft to find your "niche:"

- What am I talking about all the time?
- What is unique to me and can be found in my ideal customer?
- What can I talk about with a five-year plan?
- What value can I give when setting myself up on a blog?
- How can I show my spirit and beliefs online?
- How can I improve my website and landing page to reach my niche?

Appendix 2

Book Proposal Sample
Three Husbands and a Thousand Boyfriends

A book proposal is your case for the salability and marketability of your manuscript. It is a document that convinces editors, agents, and publishing companies, as well as the media and other important contacts, of the viability of your project.

You have the opportunity to submit sample chapters and hone your voice. Within this document, you develop a description of your target audience and prepare a tool to discuss and fine-tune your book. It is a roadmap to prepare for your author journey, a to-do list for your step-by-step approach to marketing.

The book proposal is a sales tool you use to seek an advance when offered a contract by a publisher, your chance to be a professional. You "paint a picture" of the goals you will accomplish on your path to publication.

The following book proposal, beginning with the legend (explanatory guide), is a sample of the categories you must use when writing your own. I wrote it for you using samples from my second memoir, *Three Husbands and a Thousand Boyfriends.*

I've selected each category for a reason and listed them in the order requested by publishing companies. Even if you don't pitch editors or agents for a traditional publishing contract, this book proposal format helps you plan your marketing campaign to promote you and your book.

If you write memoir or nonfiction, these six reasons explain why you need a book proposal to help you obtain what you want:

- Earn a publishing contract.
- Recognize whether you have or don't have a winning book.
- Learn about publisher expectations.
- Identify your target audience.
- Reach your target audience.
- Build exposure for your book.

Your book proposal format is an outline for you to organize the content of your book, a promise to write a quality book. You will include a competitive analysis to differentiate your title.

By understanding what "hooks" the reader in the beginning of your work, you can prepare early for your marketing and promotional efforts. You supply ample teasers to entice the editor, agent, or marketing person to read your proposal and consider a partnership. The book proposal follows.

Legend

Overview

- Why Three Husbands and a Thousand Boyfriends is different
- What readers will learn
- The purpose of this book

The Author

- Who is Patricia L. Brooks
- Mission
- Biography
- Current workshops
- Awards received

- Credentials
- Organizational memberships

Audiences
- Target, primary, secondary, fringe

Marketing and Promotion
- Website/blog
- Social media
- Speaking
- Publicity/public relations
- Online sales
- Special sales
- Retail store sales
- Book clubs
- Magazines
- Awards
- Book reviews
- Online articles
- Traditional radio
- Internet radio
- Television

Competitive Analysis
- Love addiction
- Women and violence

Table of Contents

Samples

Overview

Three Husbands and a Thousand Boyfriends is my second memoir. It tells my story of love addiction and domestic violence, trauma, recovery, and post-traumatic stress. After a tumultuous two-year relationship, my most ardent abuser assaulted me for the final time. I was taken by ambulance to the emergency room to fight for my life. I catapulted immediately into the deepest throes of post-traumatic stress, as decades of trauma began to surface. I share my story of forgiveness, growth, and recovery in this work to help other women who still suffer.

With tender detail, I show how I longed for a better life while still clinging to old habits. I went to the edge of death's door to find myself, finally accepting my part in the chaos of love addiction. Through my story of survival, other victims of domestic violence or love addiction will be inspired to seek a life of recovery and not to give up. Post-traumatic stress recovery is slow and arduous. I learned it comes with high alert, intense awareness, and nightmares, yet is an opportunity to become aware of what my healing difficulties showed me. I finally understood that, to live with post-traumatic stress, I needed to maintain hope and continue on despite the difficulties. Eventually, it helped me find hope and forgiveness.

Why Three Husbands and a Thousand Boyfriends *is different*

Three Husbands and a Thousand Boyfriends is different from other memoirs on trauma and post-traumatic stress because, in it, I disclose my personal story of abuse and recovery stemming from love addiction. Most others address only one or two of these topics. I tried to control the situation, but like any addiction, I was hooked. While faced with a debilitating sense of failure, I somehow acknowledged my "addiction to love" was coupled with a rush to chaos. Only God's grace helped me.

This memoir shares my spiritual journey to trust myself again, which I began after individual and group therapies. It is a healing story I could not have imagined on my own. It covers betrayal, renewal, and forgiveness. At my rawest point in this recovery, I nurtured my true self and my passion for writing to find out I was a survivor.

After years of emotional and psychological abuse, I offer courage and hope to anyone who may have this secret life or knows someone who does. What happened to me, what I did to myself, how I survived, and how I thrive today motivate the reader. This is my important story of hope. By letting go of my guilt and not claiming the shame sent my way, I was eventually freed. Here is a window into my forgiveness for "The Enemy" (my abuser) and myself.

What Readers Will Learn

With each chapter, readers will learn what love addiction is and what it means. This is a heartfelt book, a full-bore foray into what it feels like to be controlled emotionally and psychologically, even before physical abuse threatens life. Readers can talk about love addiction and reckon with domestic violence in the open.

The book builds on acts of early abuse and trauma to full-blown domestic violence. It later shows the aftermath in hope and recovery. My work is supported by the Arizona Coalition to End Sexual and Domestic Violence's information noting women are victims of violent crime ten times as much as believed or reported. Readers begin to understand what can be done to change the scenario. Violence against women (and men) can happen to anyone, anytime. My story illustrates that the stereotypical woman with no education, no career, with no money and nowhere to go is not the only one in this prison.

The Purpose of This Book

The purpose of this memoir is to give hope and inspiration to the many women who suffer in silence, and to show it is possible to survive and thrive. The goal is to help others. *Three Husbands and a Thousand Boyfriends* includes thoughts I wrote in my journal during my healing process, emanating from my subconscious. My conversations with God show my spiritual path. The book's purpose will be accomplished when readers who have suffered abuse are strong enough to journal their own story to heal.

The Author

Mission

My mission is to enhance the reader's appreciation of recovery from post-traumatic stress due to trauma, violence, and love addiction, and to understand and value all facets of domestic violence and its impact on women and our society.

Patricia L. Brooks

As a gifted young woman teeming with hope, passion, and ambition, I started my adult life with enthusiasm and a secret. I quickly hid my love addiction and lived just under the radar with post-traumatic stress. The emotional and psychological abuse encountered in two short marriages, which ended before age thirty, began to show in other ways such as in my personal and business relationships with other people.

I went through years of therapy. I began bringing back some sense of normalcy to my existence. My awareness of the severity of my condition rose as I moved closer to physical abuse. It was a long journey home.

I took healing steps in therapy and evaluated my incidents of trauma and potential growth. I slowly found psychological and emotional wellbeing. By offering hope and inspiration in this book, and a view of my spiritual transformation, I showed by soul. My heart's connection to God is revealed. My words encompass courage, faith, hope, self-love, and forgiveness. When all else was stripped from me, I reached deep to seek God's grace. I came back to life with the writing of this memoir.

Biography

I founded the Scottsdale Society of Women Writers in September 2005. I continue to maintain this group of more than seventy women by serving as their president. With professional speakers and an informative dinner meeting for women writers, I have earned their respect as a mentor and leader. By participating in book festivals, workshops, critique groups, and attending national writing conferences, I've inspired other writers.

Write the Memoir You're Afraid to Write

My first memoir, *Gifts of Sisterhood: Journey from Grief to Gratitude,* opened the door to present workshops on dealing with the grief process. This book earned the prestigious Arizona Authors Association Literary Contest Nonfiction award.

My second memoir and focus of this proposal, *Three Husbands and a Thousand Boyfriends,* affords me the opportunity to speak to Arizona legislators, law advocates, law enforcement, domestic violence survivors, therapists, church groups, and the community at large.

My third memoir, *Sick as My Secrets,* accompanies me to churches and recovery/treatment centers, where I present on the topic is alcoholism. I have also spoken to the Arizona Legislature on this topic and have done podcasts on addiction. Unfortunately, this disease is increasing, especially in younger women experiencing more job stress, multitasking, pressure, and competition.

As co-founder of Brooks Goldmann Publishing Company, LLC, I serve as a book shepherd on all facets of book publishing and marketing. My mission is to enhance the spirit of the writer's journey. I speak on writing, publishing, and marketing-related topics with my books. www.brooksgoldmannpublishing.com

Current Workshops

With *Three Husbands and a Thousand Boyfriends,* I present my "What Love's Not" workshop. I provide attendees with my perspective and experience on love addiction, domestic violence, and post-traumatic stress and how they all relate. I tell stories to encourage growth and healing and offer solutions in an interactive format.

Through my workshops, I enjoy the privilege of mentoring those who want to take the same path, learning the writing craft and publishing business. I have been teaching and speaking for more than thirty years in bookstores, libraries, the client's venue, and other locations.

My other popular workshops include:
- Write the Memoir You're Afraid to Write
- Publish with Marketing in Mind
- Publish Yourself as the Expert
- Journey from Grief to Gratitude

Awards Received

- Arizona Authors Association Literary Contest Nonfiction Award for her first memoir, *Gifts of Sisterhood: Journey from Grief to Gratitude*
- Named to Who's Who Amongst America's Teachers
- Outstanding Speaker Award, Arizona Small Business Association
- Arizona District Contest Winner, Toastmasters International

Credentials

- Facilitator on writing memoir for the Virginia G. Piper Center for Creative Writing at Arizona State University
- Adjunct Faculty Associate, Arizona State University, W. P. Carey School of Business, and the Osher Lifelong Learning Institute
- Master's Degree in Organizational Management (MAOM) in 1993, Bachelor's Degree in Business Management (BAM) in 1990
- The Advanced Toastmasters (ATM) designation, www.toastmastersinternational.org
- Community activist and speaker for Arizona Coalition to End Sexual and Domestic Violence (AZCESDV), www.acesdv.org
- Small business owner since 1996, home-based publishing consulting business, www.brooksgoldmannpublishing.com

Organizational Memberships
- President and founder of Scottsdale Society of Women Writers (SSWW), 2005 to present, www.scottsdalesocietyofwomenwriters.com
- Member and Writers Circle speaker, Arizona Authors Association (AAA), 2000 to present, www.azauthors.com
- Member and annual speaker, Phoenix Writers Club (PWC), 2000 to present, www.phoenixwritersclub.com
- Member and national conference attendee, Willamette Writers Club (WW), 2010 to present, www.willamettewriters.com
- Member, Speaker Bureau, Arizona Coalition to End Sexual and Domestic Violence (AZCESDV), 1996 to present

Audiences

Domestic violence eventually affects everyone in the United States, whether us personally, our children, or our grandchildren. We can all be the voice for change.

The following information is from AZCESDV's U.S. reports:
- Every nine seconds, a woman is assaulted or beaten in the United States.
- Domestic violence is the leading cause of injury to women in the United States.
- Every day, more than three women are murdered by their husbands or boyfriends.
- Upwards of twenty-five percent of the women in the United States will be assaulted in their lifetimes.

Health, wellness, safety, and serenity are of great interest to most women and to me. My desire to understand my spiritual quest and transformation is an asset to my audiences. Many women join me on this path. They are like me, so I target these women first.

Target audience: Women who currently suffer from violence or brutality in any form are the main reader target. They want to feel they are not alone and believe they can survive, recover, and thrive from violence and/or an abusive situation.

Primary purchasers: Women who have suffered violent behavior at the hand of a perpetrator or know somebody who deserves hope. This group knows coercive control through emotional and psychological abuse. In many ways, they are the most vulnerable.

Secondary purchaser: Readers interested in how abuse and violence affect a female family member or friend who has survived violence or continues to suffer. This group is wide open, from all rungs of society, races, and levels of education.

Fringe audience: Broad spectrum of the public who want to learn more about trauma, recovery, and the force of post-traumatic stress on our society and social environments. This audience includes anyone who wants to learn to recognize the symptoms of this disorder with regard to violence and abuse in our society.

Marketing and Promotion

My commitment strategy follows these media categories for this campaign. My brand represents who I am, who I show myself to be in the book, and how the book offers hope and ideas to the reader. The book's focus and audience appeal are part of this equation.

Website/Blog

- Offer blog posts on trauma, domestic violence recovery, and love addiction
- Link to other professional websites in the trauma and recovery fields
- Contact bloggers targeting recovery from trauma, violence, and spirituality to guest blog

Social Media/YouTube/Podcasts

- Extensively use Facebook, Instagram, LinkedIn, and Goodreads
- Develop a Facebook author page
- Participate in YouTube videos and podcasts, and post them on my website

Speaking

- Target recovery and addiction industry professionals
- University sororities, and high school wellness programs
- Churches, conferences, and retreats in the field of recovery

Publicity/Public Relations

- To start, pursue feature stories in major Arizona, California, and Nevada newspapers
- Write columns for several Phoenix newspapers to get my story in another format
- Contact Arizona's Senior Living newspaper, the Scottsdale Independent, The Arizona Republic, and the Arizona Progress & Gazette, regarding a column on my themes

Online Sales

- Offer my book in e-book and print versions on Amazon in the memoir/psychology genres
- Use YouTube videos, podcasts, and webinars, to promote various aspects of my talks
- Contact mental health/psychology websites to reference my link

Special Sales

- Contact stores carrying titles on Christian and Jewish religion, spiritual and holistic wellness, and health
- Expand into therapists' offices, health spas, and wellness organizations
- Contact treatment centers/recovery homes to buy the book for their clients
- Seek out book festivals that welcome memoir/nonfiction authors

Retail Store Sales

- Pursue outlets carrying spiritual titles such as Costco, Walmart, Sam's Club, and Target.
- Contact major independent western U.S. bookstores such as Powell's Books in Portland, Oregon; Changing Hands in Tempe, Arizona; the Elliot Bay Book Company in Seattle, Washington; and The Tattered Cover in Denver, Colorado, for in-store appearances.
- Pursue twelve-step program recovery and spiritual/faith-based bookstores such as Faith in Recovery in Palm Desert, California; and the Gifts Anon bookstore in Scottsdale, Arizona.

Book Clubs

- Investigate local book clubs for memoir readers.
- Contact book clubs online and plan Zoom meetings.
- Solicit memoir book clubs in major cities throughout the country using:
    - www.bookbrowse.com
    - www.readinggroupguides.com
    - www.wallstreetjournal.com
    - www.usatoday.com

Magazines

- Develop informative articles on the issue of women and violent crime.
- Author articles for *Psychology Today*, *Health & Fitness*, and *AARP* magazines.
- Seek placement locally with In Recovery Magazine and Together AZ Newspaper.

Awards

- Compete for local and national awards for women authors in memoir and nonfiction.
- Advocate online for domestic violence awareness.
- Seek recognition in the publishing arena for nonfiction.

Book Reviews

- Solicit book reviews from magazines and newspapers locally and nationally.
- Brand my image as the "go-to book" for love addiction, domestic violence, and post-traumatic recovery for women.
- Use the book reviews as promotional tools on my website.

Online Articles

- Submit e-zine articles to appropriate markets to continue branding the book.
- Present myself as the expert in love addiction, domestic violence, and post-traumatic stress.
- Build the brand consistently with e-zine articles and other blog post requests.

Traditional Radio

- Contact National Public Radio, Channel 8, KAET, Arizona State University.
- Contact Books & Co., Eight World, host Alberto Rios, National Public Radio, www.npr.org.

Internet Radio

- Seek stations looking for new books on trending topics impacting women.
- Pursue interviews with established contacts:
  - ArtistFirst Radio, www.artistsfirst.com
  - BlogTalkRadio, www.blogtalktradio.com
  - WritersFM, www.writersfm.com
  - IHeartRadio, www.iheart.com

Television

- Reach out to local television stations with shows that highlight women's issues.
- Deliver media packets to the following and follow-up:
  - Sonoran Living, Channel 15, the ABC 15, www.abc15.com
  - AZ TV Channel 13, Prescott, Arizona, https://localfirstaz.com
  - God Show with Pat McMahon, https://starworldwidernetworks.com
  - The Arizona Midday show on Channel 12, NBC, www.12news.com
- Pursue national campaign exposure with a recommended, affordable press agent.

Competitive Analysis

Love Addiction

- *I just woke up dead: a memoir*. Sex, drugs, alcohol, and addiction are the horrendous threads of this book. While I address the same topics, I also take you to my soul and describe more intensely the battles that took over my life.
  - By Justin Donner, author, and Layne Dungan, editor
- *Men-ipulatation A Memoir of Addiction and Recovery*. This book shows the depths of addiction in the pinnacle of society. My book delivers a similar journey that can happen to the person you least expect.
  - By Monica Sarli and Denise Donning
- *Love Hunger: A Harrowing Journey from Sex Addiction to True Fulfillment*. A book of hope and redemption after the bondage of a double life with desperate loneliness and sexual obsession. This author shares a story of courage and faith similar to mine yet leaves me free to show the woman's perspective.
  - By David Kyle Foster
- *Love Sick: A Woman's Journey Through Sexual Addiction*. This book has a good message about sexual addiction and learning to value yourself after a rollercoaster life of destruction. In comparison, my book goes deeper into the issues of shame and guilt. My story opens the reader up to their inner conflicts in sexual addiction.
  - By Sue W. Silverman

Women and Violence

- *I am Just a Woman: My story of domestic violence.* This is a brutally honest and engaging first-person account addressing the question, "Why does she stay?" In comparison, my memoir takes on that same question for the independent woman with no children who stays in a relationship even though she is not financially dependent.
    - By Lucy Johnson
- *I Am Not Your Victim: Anatomy of Domestic Violence.* Their book gives us the evolution of domestic violence in a long marriage, including mishaps by the police and the courts. In my book, I show you how domestic violence grew over a lifetime through my many relationships, culminating in one with physical violence.
    - By Beth Sipe and Evelyn J. Hall
- *The Beaten Path.* This book gives the reader blood, bruises, broken promises, and 911 calls from a woman overpowered and controlled. My story is similar. I take it one step further and give the reader my part in all of it and why I forgave myself for my love addiction and the chaos.
    - By Shelley Walden
- *Crazy Love.* A recovering alcoholic meets the charming man with a sorted past like her own, and they are drawn together. While experiencing his control, she leaves her job and fights to stay in graduate school. Her story is my story except I finished graduate school during my final abusive relationship. I share the revelations I found to make sense of what happened.
    - By Lesley M. Steinor

Table of Contents

    Sharing My Story
    Chapter 1   I Should Have Gone to Woodstock
    Chapter 2   Day of Reckoning
    Chapter 3   Love Addicted
    Chapter 4   Beginning of the End
    Chapter 5   Sojourner Center
    Chapter 6   The Terror in PTS
    Chapter 7   Disconnection
    Chapter 8   Trials and Tribulations
    Chapter 9   Spiritual Transformation
    Chapter 10   Dear Nicole
    Chapter 11   Take My Car
    Chapter 12   Wishes Do Come True
    Epilogue
    About the Author
    Author's Request
    Services and Resources

Samples

Chapter 1: I Should Have Gone to Woodstock

    The support I needed to make the best decision for marriage was not available or, if it was, I did not seek it. I was torn somewhere in the middle between taking a chance at a new lifestyle and following my gut that said slow down. I was suffocating by it all.

Chapter 3: Love Addicted

    I am not sure when I crossed the line and ramped up the love addiction, but for the ten years, I was attracted to mostly African-American men. I was consumed by the mysterious and challenging, losing sight of who really was the right guy for me. My social life had a narrow focus and my time with friends was minimal.

Chapter 4: The Beginning of the End

An oozing warmth on my neck felt like the hot oil treatments I had done to my hair, but it was my blood. Reaching up, I felt the throbbing part of my head and realized I was cut open. I feared he would finish the job this time.

Chapter 6: Terror

I was trapped in my own home like a rat in the hull of a ship. I sensed the danger around me as soon as he broke through the rear door. I felt helpless, adrift at sea in a small boat where the sharks were circling.

Chapter 8: Trials and Tribulations

Ten stitches in the back of my head and fearing for my life do not qualify me for a consultation with the city attorney prior to meeting with the judge. My whole case is prepared from my journal notes, the police report, and the city attorney's brief call to me.

Chapter 9: Spiritual Transformation

My struggles to trust and to pray with conviction were very real. I had a tough time focusing on God to get to a deep and quiet place. The chaos in my soul did not end until I found answers that came only after long times in prayer.

Acknowledgements

I required an army of friends, proofreaders, my critique group, my editor, and my husband to mold this book to what it is meant to be. My gratitude for this team knows no bounds.

To my husband, Earl L. Goldmann, who is always optimistic about what I am writing and eager to proofread what I produce. He is my rock. On this journey to publish a fourth book, he has always been there for me, and for that, I am grateful. I support his writing endeavors too.

Secondly, thank you to my friend, colleague, and book shepherd, Ann Videan, who painstakingly edited this nonfiction work with much care and diligence. Her keen eye kept this book focused. She also added her expertise to the layout and design of the book to take this project to fruition.

Thank you as well to Kristi Wayland of Electronic Ink AZ for a book cover that entices the reader. And bookmarks that complement the book cover and add to my marketing plans.

Finally, thank you to my critique group members, Darlene Ziebell, Rose Garlasco, and Courtney Schrauben Haik, who spent countless hours over the past several years giving me feedback on these pages. I deeply appreciate their friendship and encouragement. They helped me define my purpose for the book, both with their feedback and challenges.

Thank you to the women of Scottsdale Society of Women Writers, my personal friends and workshop attendees who appreciate my expertise on the topic. You are extremely important to me, even more than you realize.

A final thank-you to all of you reading this work. May you find that your own story emerges after finishing these pages and moves forward to a full manuscript.

Author's Request

It is my hope you will share your feedback now that you have taken this journey with me to visualize your success as a memoir writer.

Please send comments on the book and your reaction as a witness to the world of writing memoirs. I would love to hear from you, either with a review on www.Amazon.com, Goodreads, or in a personal email.

Thank you for the feedback and God bless.

Patricia L. Brooks
www.brooksgoldmannpublishing.com
www.amazon.com

Write the Memoir You're Afraid to Write
www.writethememoiryouareafraiddtowrite.com
ISBN: 979-8-9915962-0-6 (paperback)

Write the Memoir You're Afraid to Write

Book Club Discussion Questions

Eight to ten are recommended to begin a discussion.

1. What was the author's intent or objective for the book?
2. Did this nonfiction book entertain, educate, or explain something?
3. What was the most surprising thing you learned about memoir writing?
4. How did the author explore the topic?
5. Did the author effectively use historical resources or individual experiences?
6. Did the book challenge or change your perspective on writing memoir?
7. Did you find the book easy to read and the activities fun?
8. Did the author appear biased on the topic in any chapter?
9. Did you learn something new? What was it, and was it helpful?
10. What was your favorite part of the book?
11. What was your least favorite part of the book?
12. What did you think of the writing?
13. Did this book inspire you to explore the topic more?
14. Of all the information in the book, what impacted you the most?

About the Author

Patricia L. Brooks, MAOM
Award-winning Author, Speaker, Advocate, and Consultant

Patricia L. Brooks is an award-winning author of three memoirs. Her newest work is titled *Write the Memoir You're Afraid to Write*. This nonfiction book complements her workshop, encouraging and inspiring "wannabe" memoir writers and story tellers.

She published her first memoir, *Gifts of Sisterhood*, as a tribute to her sister who passed away from lung cancer, and to understand grief. Two other memoirs followed: *Three Husbands and a Thousand Boyfriends* is an inspiring story of her recovery from love addiction and surviving domestic violence. *Sick as My Secrets* is a candid look at her courageous journey of sobriety through alcohol abuse, and how she now lives her life well.

Patricia added Brooks Goldmann Publishing Company, LLC, as a consultant, to her offerings in 2007. She guides potential authors through the maze of independent publishing by putting a team together to make independent publishing possible.

As a speaker, Patricia presents on topics such as writing memoirs/nonfiction books, independent publishing, and book marketing. She also speaks on grief, recovery, love addiction, and domestic violence awareness. Her mission is to enhance the attendee's experience and to help others.

Patricia continues to serve as a university adjunct-faculty associate. More than twenty-five years ago she became affiliated with Arizona State University and the Maricopa County Community College District. She holds a Master's Degree in Organizational Management (MAOM), a Bachelor's Degree in Business Management, the Advanced Toastmasters designation, and was named to Who's Who Amongst America's Teachers.

Before book publication, she authored articles and short stories, edited university curriculum, and expanded her career of seminar presentations. Patricia has inspired and contributed to the development of many successful writers. As president of the phenomenally successful Scottsdale Society of Women Writers, she continues to support its growth. She is also a member of the

Arizona Authors Association and the Phoenix Writers Club. She resides in Old Town Scottsdale, Arizona, with her author husband, Earl L. Goldmann. They enjoy the culture and vibe of the area.

Contact Patricia for speaking engagements or a consultation on writing or publishing:

Call/text: 480-250-5556
Personal: patricia@plbrooks.com
Business: info@brooksgoldmannpublishing.com
Website: www.brooksgoldmannpublishing.com